The Bruce Lee Story

Editors: Mike Lee and Jack Vaughn
Graphic Design: Sergio Onaga

Photos courtesy of Linda Lee's private collection, Rainbow Publications, Inc. and Ohara Publications, Inc. Additional photos: Warner Brothers, Golden Harvest Films, Twentieth Century-Fox, Concord Productions, and Paramount Pictures.

Library of Congress Catalog Card Number: 88-63487
ISBN 0-89750-121-7
Second Printing 1989

OHARA 🄿 PUBLICATIONS, INC.
BURBANK, CALIFORNIA

by Linda Lee and Tom Bleecker

Dedication

This book is dedicated to Brandon Bruce Lee and Shannon Emery Lee—the two people who brought to Bruce more joy, more love, and more fulfillment than all the wings of fame and fortune—that they might know the rich legacy which is theirs alone.

Acknowledgements

I would like to acknowledge the presence in my life of several people who are particularly wonderful human beings.

My mother, Vivian Dickinson, has come to my aid in all ways at all times. I love you, Mom.

My sister Joan cared for my children as her own particularly in the early days after Bruce's death. Thanks, Sis.

I must mention collectively all the great people in my large extended family. I have never stood alone because I have had the love and support of all these wonderful people.

Not too many people have as good a friend as I do in Rebu Hui. We have spent countless hours together through all the good times and bad, and she has always prayed for my happiness and peace of mind.

Adrian Marshall, my lawyer, has smoothed the often-bumpy legal way. His attention to the legal aspects of Bruce's life and death have allowed me to pursue a trouble-free life-style.

My thanks to all the members of the JKD community who have sought to protect Bruce's image often in the face of adversity. Thanks for continuing to find your own way instead of following blindly.

My appreciation to all the people at Ohara Publications, especially the owner and Bruce's good friend, M. Uyehara. Ohara has always given Bruce journalistic respect and has gone to battle for him on numerous occasions. Others at Ohara who have contributed greatly to the publication of this book include Geri Simon, Sergio Onaga, Mike Lee, and Jack Vaughn.

My deep appreciation to the countless fans and admirers of Bruce. You have helped spread Bruce's message around the world and continue to do so. I wish I could thank each of you individually, but I hope I have answered most of your questions in this book.

—*Linda Lee*

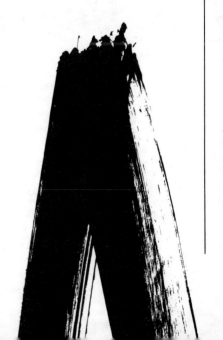

Noted educator and patriot, grandmaster Jhoon Rhee is generally hailed as the "Father of American tae kwon do."

The name Bruce Lee stands out for popularizing martial arts throughout the world. When I introduced *tae kwon do*, the Korean martial art, to America in 1956, it was practically unknown to the America public. Bruce Lee's movies, beginning with *The Green Hornet* TV series in 1966, to the famous 1973 smash box office hit *Enter the Dragon*, one of the most exciting motion pictures, created immense interest in the martial arts.

Bruce Lee was a man of knowledge, strength, compassion and love. As one of Bruce's closest friends, I am forever grateful to him for what he did in establishing, the value of martial arts in our modern society. His untimely death at such an early age, in 1973, was not only a loss for martial arts but also for the world. Bruce Lee still lives on in our minds, for his spirit never left our hearts. I am indebted to his widow, Linda, for bringing the full story of Bruce Lee to the whole world through this book.

Bruce Lee was a true martial arts student, teacher and international leader. He paved the way for other martial artists such as Chuck Norris, Jackie Chan, Ralph Macchio, and Jean Claude Van Damme to become movie stars of our time.

I trust that this book will enlighten many people, especially martial artists, around the world. I extend my best wishes to Bruce Lee's family, daughter Shannon, son Brandon, Linda and Tom, who co-authored this book. I hope they find every success in life, and this book achieves the popularity it deserves.

—*Jhoon Rhee*

Bruce was, indeed, a unique, and rare individual. From the time I first met Bruce through Jimmy Lee, I was impressed with his balance, speed, accuracy, and power. Weighing only 145 pounds, he punched with extraordinary speed and force. Most impressive was his ability to "pop" the air when he punched. As I became more intimately acquainted with Bruce, it was obvious that he possessed qualities which were exceptional. He had learned to develop that extra inner force created by the precise synchronization of the conscious and subconscious mind, along with an individual's breath and strength, which made him superior over the highly skilled. While most people improve over the years, his movements looked just as good the first day that I met him up to the time of his death. His perfected basics never faltered. The only martial arts improvement in his life was the additional knowledge that he had acquired beyond his wing chun training.

Renowned kenpo grandmaster Ed Parker is widely regarded as the "Father of American karate."

Bruce had an uncanny ability to study and scrutinize martial artists. I remember him observing a martial artist execute a specific kick that had taken eight years to perfect. He then executed the same kick, looked equally as good the first time and better the second time around. Even though he had never done the kick before, others could not be convinced that this was true. In my opinion, his caliber of talent was one in two billion.

Beyond his ability as a martial artist, Bruce was jovial, full of wit, entertaining, and he had a knack for capturing people's attention. He seldom appeared in public without captivating an audience. In addition to having this special charismatic dominance, he was always poised, self-assured, and, on occasion, cocky. His occasional cockiness, however, was easily backed by his superior physical skills. He was opposed to traditional brainwashing and made no bones about it. He detested systems that made carbon copies of their students, and although he voiced his concepts and theories, they were unfortunately, and often, misconstrued.

Because of Bruce's exceptional abilities, Jimmy Lee sought my help. He knew that once I observed Bruce's extraordinary talent I would use my influence to help Bruce gain recognition in the movies and on television. We foresaw the future of the martial arts with Bruce as a star performer. Knowing that there would be a number of movie and TV producers at my first International Karate Championships tournament held in 1964 at Long Beach, California, I asked Bruce to demonstrate his skills. Bruce's demonstration was captured on film and after the tournament, I showed it to Bill Dozier who hired Bruce as Kato in the *Green Hornet* series. While the rest is history, I feel grateful to have been a part of Bruce's life and honored to have been asked to write this foreword for a wonderful book on his life as seen through the eyes of his wife, Linda.
                                                    —*Ed Parker*

1

The first time I saw Bruce he was standing at the end of a long hallway at Garfield High School in Seattle, Washington. I was 17 years old and a senior, he was 22 and a sophomore at the University of Washington. I was talking with several girlfriends when I looked up and said "Who is that?" He was so handsome and well-dressed, wearing a hat with a skinny brim and a long beige raincoat, he was not an ordinary sight in our school—too young to be a teacher, yet older and more sophisticated than a student. On his arm was his pretty Japanese girlfriend, who was a former graduate of Garfield High.

My Chinese girlfriend, Sue Ann Kay, replied, "Oh, that's Bruce Lee, the man I take kung fu lessons from. He's here to lecture in Mr. Wilson's class on Chinese philosophy." I was more than a little impressed as I watched him laughing and talking and throwing playful punches with some kids down the hall. It would be several months before I formally met Bruce.

Bruce spent that summer of 1963 in Hong Kong, his first trip home after his rather hasty departure in 1959. In those four years he had changed from a rebellious youth to a responsible young man who was welcomed back into the good graces of his family. I graduated from high school, took a summer job at Sears, and prepared to enter the University of Washington in the fall.

I used to kid my friend Sue Ann about that strange Chinese self-defense stuff she was studying. I had never heard the word kung fu before, and even karate and judo were relatively insignificant terms in the early 60s. Almost on a dare, Sue Ann said to me "Why don't you come to a lesson with me sometime and see what it's like?"

Classy was the word for Bruce.

Bruce and I in front of his kwoon on University Way in Seattle.

Bruce teaching a small group of students in a parking garage in his early days in Seattle.

One Sunday morning I went with her to Chinatown. We entered the building through a half-door that faced on the sidewalk, went down a flight of dingy, dark stairs, and emerged in a basement room with concrete walls, bare lightbulbs, and no other decoration. I thought, "Oh brother! What did I get myself into now?!" It would not be the last time I had such a thought.

The atmosphere in the room, however, was cheerful and active. There were about a dozen people present talking and stretching, getting ready for the class to start. Sue Ann gave the kung fu salutation to her *sifu* (instructor) Bruce and he came over to greet us. He welcomed me to the class and then began teaching. Little did I suspect that almost exactly one year from that Sunday morning I would marry Bruce Lee.

I began taking lessons regularly. Lessons were more than just learning techniques in the gym, however. There was a social element to them as well. Bruce was always a friend to his students and after training on a Sunday morning we would all go out to lunch at a Chinese restaurant. It was my introduction to real Chinese food. Up to this time Chinese food was chop suey, chow mein with crispy noodles, and sugar in my tea. The first time Bruce saw me put sugar in Chinese tea he practically gagged. I had my first Chinese hamburger and other small snacks called *dim sum* which are typically served at a Chinese lunch. I've been a convert ever since.

After a long joyous lunch (Bruce used to make me laugh till I hurt) we might all go to a film at a theater in Chinatown. We would see a Japanese samurai movie, perhaps *Sanjuro* or *Zatoichi, the Blind Swordsman*, and all the while Bruce would provide a running commentary about the action. One Chinese film that we saw was *The Orphan*, the last film Bruce made before he had left Hong Kong. Before this I had barely been aware that Bruce had an acting background. He never emphasized the fact that he had been a child star in Hong Kong. Now here he was on the screen in a theater in Seattle's Chinatown. I realized that there was more to this man than I had thought.

It might seem strange that I would suddenly become immersed in Asian culture. After all I was a blonde-haired, blue-eyed girl of English and Swedish stock, born and raised in the Pacific Northwest, reared as a Protestant by a mother with strict Anglo-Saxon values. But it really wasn't all that strange as I look back on it. My high school was an inner-city school which, even back in the late 50s, was 40-percent black, 40-percent white, and 20-percent Asian. Many of my girlfriends were Japanese and Chinese. I was welcomed in their homes, as they were in mine. I even dated a half-Japanese boy for a brief time until my mom put her stamp of disapproval on that. Girlfriends were OK, but boys definitely were not—that was not

Bruce on the shores of Lake Washington.

Bruce in front of the columns of the amphitheater on the University of Washington campus where he asked me for our first date.

Bruce teaching in his kwoon on University Way. Second from left is Bruce's assistant instructor Taky Kimura. Next to him are Charlie Woo, and Sue Ann Kay.

This is me as a cheerleader at Garfield High School.

acceptable in our family. My father died when I was five years old and the raising of my older sister and me was left to my mother. It had not been an easy task and now my poor mom was to be presented with real problems.

In September of 1963, I began my freshman year at the University of Washington where Bruce was beginning his junior year as a philosophy major. Many of his kung fu students were also attending the university, which allowed us to continue our lessons on an even more frequent basis. On almost any day during lunch hour, Bruce would be holding court in the HUB (the Student Union Building). There was always a group of friends and followers seated around Bruce. He captivated everyone's attention with his philosophical dissertations, and uproarious jokes, and best of all, his magnificent demonstrations of kung fu.

In addition to attracting a lot of attention, Bruce was also gaining new students. Moreover, he had petitioned the university to allow him to give formally sanctioned exhibitions in the men's gym and so he was building his reputation through this means also. He was creating the type of sensation on campus which he would duplicate in the years to come in a much larger arena. Later, when Bruce gave demonstrations at the university, he recruited some of his most devout students from the ranks of the sports teams. He was highly regarded by football players and other athletes whose first reaction had always been that this little Chinese guy couldn't possibly touch them. The range of people that Bruce came in contact with at the University of Washington was a microcosm of what was to come. He had the respect of professors who cared little about martial arts as well as members of the student body who respected a highly trained body.

Bruce was creating quite a sensation with me, too. I was enrolled as a pre-med student and my science classes were intense. However, I always found time to sit around in the HUB and, as time went on, I began to cut a class now and then so I could be around Bruce. My freshman year at college nearly turned into a disaster. Studying and becoming captivated by Bruce were not compatible. But at this time I didn't realize what was happening and besides, I didn't think Bruce would ever consider me romantically anyway. He was so dashing and charming, he could have had his choice of dates. Regardless, I was having fun just being part of his kung fu group.

One of our favorite things to do at school was to go over to the large, rectangular grass area used for outdoor concerts. It was fenced-in by trees and beautiful Grecian columns on one end. The whole group of us would go there to practice kung fu with plenty of space and soft grass to land on. One afternoon, Bruce and I were racing from one end to the other and when

Bruce and James Lee.

Bruce and Taky Kimura.

Bruce arriving in Hong Kong—his first trip home after four years in the United States, summer of 1963.

we got away from the group he tackled me to the ground. I thought he was going to show me a new maneuver, but instead, he held me down and when I stopped laughing, he asked me if I wanted to go to dinner at the Space Needle. I hesitated a moment, thinking that was a pretty expensive place for all of us to go, and I said, "You mean all of us?" And he replied, "No, only you and me." I was speechless, although I must have managed to say, "Yes!"

October 25, 1963—the evening of our first date. Bruce picked me up in his black '57 Ford at my girlfriend's house. My mom would never have let me go out with him alone so I just skirted that issue for the time being. I had borrowed my friend's dress and coat because I didn't have anything appropriate to wear to a fancy restaurant. The Space Needle had been built for the 1962 Seattle World's Fair and its observation deck and revolving restaurant towered over the city. Classy was the word for Bruce. When he arrived for our date he was wearing a black Italian silk suit, purple shirt, and black tie. His hair was slicked back on the sides and a curl dangled on his forehead. He looked so much like my idol George Chakaris, the leader of the Sharks in *West Side Story*, that I was instantly charmed.

I was nervous about being able to carry on a conversation with this gorgeous man now that I was alone with him and did not have the security of the group. A new element had been introduced into our relationship. My fears were needless, however, as Bruce put me completely at ease. He always could talk enough for the both of us, and even in later years, whenever I was at a loss for words, he would fill in the gaps. Over dinner, I was fascinated with Bruce's life story and with his plans for the future. In my mind it occurred to me to ask him why he had singled me out for this romantic dinner, but I was too shy to bring it up.

To complete the evening, Bruce presented me with a memento. It was a tiny Scandinavian troll doll, a kewpie doll. Bruce had gone to the trouble of braiding the hair into pigtails. I was delighted because I knew instantly the significance of the gift. It looked just like me when I would walk into the Student Union Building with hair wet and in pigtails after my swimming class. Bruce was the best gift-giver—he always gave the personal touch when he didn't have money as well as when he could afford to be more lavish. Our date ended with a light kiss when Bruce dropped me off at my house. It was the end of the perfect evening.

That fall of 1963, Bruce moved the Jun Fan Gung Fu Institute to 4750 University Way near the university campus. He was now convinced that he could make his livelihood as a kung fu instructor, and his future plans included opening

JUN FAN GUNG FU INSTITUTE

振 藩 國 術 館

會
員
證

MEMBERSHIP CARD.

Name 姓名 *LINDA EMERY*

Address 地址 *2332 11TH E.*

Signature *Linda Emery*

(President)

No. 0008

**PERMANENT
MEMBER
RANK**

1	5
2	6
3	7
4	8

My membership card in the Jun Fan Gung Fu Institute.

As a college freshman, I studied "gung fu" from Bruce. Here I am standing in front of his gym on University Way.

Bruce in Seattle—1963.

schools in various locations around the country. The new space was 3,000 square feet and occupied the entire ground floor of an apartment building. It had a large community-type shower room, about 10x15 feet with numerous shower heads coming out of the walls. The space must have been planned as a gym of some sort for the use of only one sex at a time presumably. Bruce liked to turn all the showers on at once and turn it into a steamroom.

There was a room in the back of the gym which Bruce used as his bedroom. He had a beautiful set of teakwood furniture which he had brought back from Hong Kong the previous summer. The funny thing about Bruce's bedroom was that there were no windows. When you came in the rear entrance there was also no light switch near the door. You had to stumble across the room in pitch blackness to find the light. You could sleep forever in the room because the sun never appeared to let you know the time of day. Sometimes I'd pick up Bruce for school in the morning and he'd still be asleep because the room would be so dark he didn't have a clue what time it was.

This was the only time in our lives that Bruce and I got hooked on a soap opera. It became a ritual. Every day after school we'd run back to his place and get there in time for *General Hospital*. Then Bruce would take me out to dinner across the street at a Chinese restaurant where he knew the cook, old Ah Sam. Almost every time we had the same thing—oyster sauce beef and shrimp with black-bean sauce. It was great—my taste buds were becoming Chinese. Unfortunately I would have to go home and eat a full dinner again with my family. My mother was beginning to think I was anorexic because I ate such small portions. I had always been a skinny kid and she was determined that I eat a full-course meal every night. Since she did not know I was dating Bruce, it was getting to be a sticky situation and I was at a loss as to how to handle it. I didn't like deceiving my mom but I liked even less the idea of not being able to see Bruce, and I knew she had very strong feelings about that subject. It was one of those issues in life for which there is no satisfactory solution and so I put it on the back burner for the time being. Since Bruce and I were almost constantly together, it took quite a bit of maneuvering and a little help from my friends. This couldn't last forever, of course, and it would shortly become an explosive situation.

My school work was going right down the proverbial drain. It was not the primary focus of my attention. But Bruce didn't have any problems at all—he could whack off a philosophical essay practically during the commercials. His command of the English language was nearly perfect from a grammatical standpoint. It was certainly better than mine because he knew all the rules by heart, having learned English as a second language.

My parents—Everett and Vivian Emery.

My mother—Vivian Dickinson.

My stepfather, Pop—Willard Dickinson.

When I got in a jam and fell behind in my work, Bruce would help me write papers for my English class. He was no help at all in chemistry or calculus, but he could write. Besides, I told him it was his fault that I wasn't getting my work done. He could only smile in agreement.

While attending the University of Washington Bruce kept in touch with another close friend, James Y. Lee, a practitioner and instructor of kung fu in Oakland, California. Bruce had met James briefly in 1959 when he first came to the United States and had stayed for a few months in the Bay Area teaching cha-cha dance lessons. James and Bruce had a common interest in kung fu and they spent many hours together comparing techniques and philosophies. When Bruce moved to Seattle to attend school, he and James continued to see each other whenever possible.

By June of 1964, at the end of Bruce's junior year, he and James had made plans to open the second branch of the Jun Fan Gung Fu Institute in Oakland. Bruce had decided that he didn't really need to finish school, at least not right then, and that he would be better off implementing his well-detailed plans to open branches of his school. At the close of the school year, Bruce gave up his lease at 4750 University Way and arranged with Taky Kimura to take over his classes as head instructor of the Seattle branch of the Jun Fan Gung Fu Institute. He had his furniture and other belongings shipped to Oakland, and he sold his car because he needed the money. I watched this whirlwind of activity with trepidation, wondering how I fit into the master plan.

When I took Bruce to the airport for his departure to Oakland, I still didn't know the answer to that question. Neither did Bruce. The idea of commitment scared him to death. He wanted to be financially secure before undertaking the responsibility of a wife and family. We had talked about marriage, but later, some distant time down the road.

As he got ready to board the plane, Bruce could read the feelings on my face. He said simply, ''I'll be back,'' and then he was gone. I felt like the bottom had dropped out of my life. What if I never saw him again? What if he went on to bigger and better things and memories of me got lost in the shuffle? These thoughts raced through my mind. We had not made a commitment to each other. Bruce did not want to make a commitment until he had ''established'' himself. He felt it was important to have a financial foundation before he could commit to the idea of a wife and children. In retrospect, I'm glad he didn't decide to wait forever, otherwise there might never have been a Brandon and Shannon.

The summer of 1964 was a summer of letters. Bruce wrote me daily all through the summer expressing his desires and

Bruce in the Kato years. The Chinese symbol under his English signature means "Dragon."

Bruce working out in the hills of Hong Kong
—1963.

concerns. I had rented a post office box in downtown Seattle where I received Bruce's letters because I couldn't have them sent to my home. I felt there was no need to tell my mom about Bruce now since he might never return.

Finally, Bruce wrote that he wanted me with him and would return to Seattle to get me. If it sounds like a one-sided decision, I guess it was. I *knew* I wanted to be with this man forever. It was a matter of Bruce deciding if he could handle the idea of marriage. Being separated for two-and-a-half months gave him time to think it over. Of course I was happy, elated, ecstatic. Except . . . there was the problem of my family, especially my mom. This was going to be a very delicate situation full of anger and hurt. Bruce was very concerned about my family's reaction. In fact it was one of the reasons why he had hesitated so long. He realized, even better than I did, that when you marry a woman, you marry the family as well. He didn't want to enter our marriage with the black cloud of family rejection hanging over us. But we had ducked this issue for so long that now it was very complicated. Being young and in love, however, love won out, and we decided to face the music. I felt terrible about it but I knew that marrying Bruce was the right thing to do.

Bruce and I decided on the coward's way out. We'd get married, run away to Oakland, then call my mom and tell her. A friend of mine had done this a couple of months earlier and after the dust had settled, everyone had survived. It was a lousy plan, and I was scared. Bruce had more of a sense of history and a better idea of how a mother would react, and he assured me that everything would be OK. He would be proven correct. He had never been happy about concealing our relationship, but he had agreed to go along with it throughout our courtship.

Bruce returned to Seattle on Wednesday, August 12, and we went to the King County Courthouse to apply for a marriage license. Aside from a mandatory three-day waiting period, there was one major problem we hadn't foreseen. First of all, we didn't know that the names of those who apply for marriage licenses are published in the newspaper. Secondly, old aunties are the type of people who read the Vital Statistics section of the paper. Specifically, my Aunt Sally, who proceeded to call my mom to tell her that a Linda C. Emery and a Bruce J.F. Lee had declared their intent to marry. The cat was not only out of the bag, but was sitting on my mother's lap.

My mother called a family powwow. My aunt and uncle came down from Everett. Bruce and I were called on the carpet to explain the situation. There was nothing to do but confess our plans. All day long the family tried to dissuade us from doing this foolish thing. Their argument was that it wouldn't

hurt to wait, and would give us time to examine our feelings. But Bruce and I had already done that—it was the family that needed the time. My mother felt hurt and angered that I, her baby and straight-A student for whom she had such high hopes, was about to run off with a ne'er-do-well Chinese kung fu instructor. As I write this, with children older than I was when I presented my mother with this information, I can readily understand her feelings. What hurt the most, of course, was that I had deceived her. Neither Bruce nor I was proud of the fact.

There was never a question about whether or not the family liked Bruce. They just didn't know him. The big issue was the interracial aspect. They felt we would suffer the slings and arrows of society's prejudice, and our children likewise. My aunt and uncle were very religious and they thought the mixing of the races was an abomination. On the contrary, I felt strongly that God would bless our union. My mom was more hurt than anything else.

One might think that because of all this turmoil our marriage got off to an inauspicious beginning. I believe it only served to strengthen our resolve to make this union work. By questioning us so thoroughly and making us explain our feelings for each other out loud, my family actually served as premarriage counselors. In the final analysis, we were more convinced than ever that we were doing the right thing.

Bruce had been on his own in the U.S. for five years and was used to making his own decisions. Also, his mother was half-Caucasian so this would not be the first time the racial barrier had been broken in his family. Bruce wrote to his family, apprising them of his plans, and they replied that, even though they wished he would marry a Chinese, they would nevertheless welcome me to the family. Bruce's letters to them were the first time they had heard of our relationship, yet they trusted his good judgment. I think they always knew that, despite his difficulties as a young person in Hong Kong, he was an intelligent person with a good sense of right and wrong in the universal sense.

Although my mom had forebodings about my future happiness, I must give her credit for making the best of the situation. What was done, was done. In the months and years that followed, she grew to love Bruce dearly and accepted him as a member of the family. She visited us often when we lived in Los Angeles and Hong Kong, and rejoiced in the births of our children Brandon and Shannon. Today I'm sure she cannot imagine that she ever had cause to worry about our happiness.

More workouts in Hong Kong.

2

"As long as I can remember I feel I have had this great creative and spiritual force within me that is greater than faith, greater than ambition, greater than confidence, greater than determination, greater than vision. It is all these combined. My brain becomes magnetized with this dominating force which I hold in my hand."

—Bruce Lee

Lee Hoi Chuen holding Bruce for his first screen appearance at the age of three months.

Bruce was born in the Year of the Dragon, in the Hour of the Dragon (between 6:00 a.m. and 8:00 a.m.) on November 27, 1940. From the beginning it was obvious he was a remarkable and unique child, with tremendous burning energy.

His city of birth was San Francisco, at the Jackson Street Hospital in Chinatown, the son of Mr. and Mrs. Lee Hoi Chuen. His father, a well-known performer with the Cantonese Opera Company of Hong Kong, was on an American tour at the time. Bruce's mother, Grace Lee, who was half German and a Catholic, christened him Lee Jun Fan, which meant "return again" because she felt he would one day return to live in the United States. One of the nurses in the hospital suggested his English name Bruce, but it was a name never used in the family until he enrolled at La Salle College in Hong Kong many years later. At home he was always called Sai Fon (Small Phoenix), a feminine name. Mr. and Mrs. Lee had lost their first son, and according to Chinese tradition when future sons are born, they are often addressed by a girl's name in order to confuse the spirits who might steal away their souls.

In all likelihood there are very few people living in the United States who could identify with Bruce's childhood home environment. In early 1941 when Bruce's parents returned to Hong Kong and the family's two-bedroom flat at 218 Nathan Road, Kowloon, the Lee household consisted of Mr. Lee, his wife Grace, Bruce's two sisters Phoebe and Agnes, his brother Peter, later to be joined by his younger brother Robert. For all intents and purposes Bruce might have done equally well had he pitched a tent on the floor of New York's Grand Central Station.

In addition to the immediate family members, the flat was home to Mr. Lee's sister-in-law and her five children. On the death of his brother, Mr. Lee, as is the Chinese custom, had taken the whole family into his own home and supported them as he would his own family. Together with the servants and the son of one of the servants, this meant that nearly 20 people were crowded into the flat, along with assorted dogs, cats, birds, and fish.

One can only imagine the nightly scene at the family dinner table, not to mention the morning scrimmage to the single bathroom. Although Bruce didn't realize it at the time, in all likelihood it was in the Nathan Road household where the seeds of jeet kune do were first planted, later to give birth to the basic concepts of efficiency, economy of motion and simplicity. In any event, I would like to suggest that more often than not Bruce's philosophical and spiritual inquiries into the basic nature of his own inner being were responded to with more relevant dialogues such as "Hurry up, Bruce, it's your turn to use the bathroom!" Regardless, Bruce's mentor, and thus his direction in life, would have to be found somewhere other than his childhood home.

It was through his father's connections that Bruce ultimately became a child film star. His father used to bring him backstage at the theaters, and often took him on tour in mainland China during school vacations. Whenever possible, Bruce hung around the set when his father was working on a film. As a young man, Bruce's father was strikingly handsome and had a very dynamic presence on stage. Bruce both loved and respected his father, perhaps even idolized, and at times even feared him. As to his own acting ability, it is clear that from the very beginning Bruce possessed a great natural talent of his own, as well as a great love of the greasepaint.

Few people have started a major film career as early as Bruce did. He was scarcely three months old when he was carried on for a part in a Chinese movie made in San Francisco, although he considered his professional screen debut as his role in *The Beginning of a Boy*, which he made in Hong Kong when he was six. He was eight when he played his second role—under the name Lee Siu Lung (Lee Little Dragon), the name by which he became best known in Hong Kong and on the Mandarin film circuit of Southeast Asia. By the time he was 18, Bruce had appeared in 20 films, including a starring role in his last film as a child star, *The Orphan*.

Whenever Bruce worked late at night or had an early morning call on the set, Bruce's mother recalls, "He liked it very much. At two o'clock in the morning, I'd call out 'Bruce, the car is here,' and he'd leap up and put on his shoes and go off very cheerfully. There was no trouble getting him up when it came to making a film. When I had to get him up for school in the mornings, however, it was quite a different story."

Although as a child Bruce both respected and loved his father, their father-son relationship was neither nurturing nor supportive. One reason is that because of his hectic schedule which often

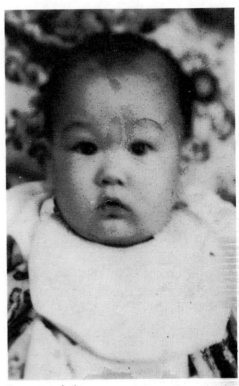

Bruce as a baby.

The Lee children. From the left: Robert, Agnes, Bruce, Peter, Phoebe.

21

Bruce's father, Lee Hoi Chuen.

The Lee family.

took him away from Hong Kong, Mr. Lee was, for the most part, an absentee parent. It is difficult to say how this affected Bruce as a child, but looking back at Bruce's adult film career I know that of all problems that Bruce faced whenever he was forced to be away on location, the greatest torment of all was being separated from his family.

In addition to being an absentee father, Lee Hoi Chuen was a licensed opium smoker. During times when he did return home to Hong Kong, he was often not mentally there for Bruce. Throughout his life Bruce rarely indulged in even the mildest alcohol drink, and I believe the true reasons for this were rooted in his upbringing as well as his desire to be physically healthy and in condition.

In the final analysis it is clear that Bruce's own personal identity, and more importantly, his direction in life, were not to be found in either his early show business career or his family life.

At school Bruce was anything but an avid student. Put in plain and simple terms, he just found it impossible to relate to the conventional format of public education, just as later in life he could not relate to conventional martial arts. Although he displayed a mild interest in history and social studies, he absolutely detested math and sciences. As his mother jokingly says, "By the time he was ten, that was as far as he could count."

After attending Chinese elementary schools, Bruce entered La Salle College at the age of 12. La Salle is a Catholic boys' school. Classes are taught in English, even though most of the boys are Chinese and have no English-speaking background, which was Bruce's case. Scholasticaly speaking, Bruce's grades at La Salle were average, at best. I believe that his frustrations at that point in his life were mounting, and as a result he repeatedly found himself in trouble at school. Bruce was not to find his life's direction in standard education. With the burning force continuing to rage inside him he did what many adolescent boys struggling for their identity do in troubled times—he turned to the streets and his peer group.

As I look back at Bruce's early years and contemplate the many thoughts he shared with me, it is clear that as a young man he was terribly frustrated by his early inability to find a spiritual guide. He needed a mentor who would assist him in finding a direction to channel this unique and incredible energy. As he so often observed in later years, "A good instructor functions as a pointer of the truth, exposing the student's vulnerability, forcing him to explore himself both internally and externally, and finally integrating himself with his being."

Back in the 1940s the British Crown Colony of Hong Kong, with the city of Kowloon and its suburbs in the New Territories, was a crowded, jostling place where people had to struggle fiercely to survive. Bruce spent his childhood there during the

Bruce's mother, Grace.

Bruce as a child actor in Hong Kong appearing in The Orphan.

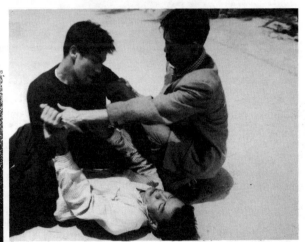

*Bruce played the role of a juvenile delinquent in
The Orphan—his last film as a child actor in
Hong Kong—approximately 1958.*

Bruce reading lines as a child actor—note the intensity on his face, a characteristic that would later manifest itself in his adult film roles.

Bruce posing on a motorcycle—an early sign of his passion for fast vehicles.

World War II Japanese occupation. He once perched above Nathan Road to shake his fist defiantly at a Japanese plane flying overhead. Moreover, he lived through the tumultuous and dangerous years following the 1949 Communist triumph in mainland China when a constant stream of refugees, many fleeing famine conditions, poured into the colony.

Gangs of young Chinese boys roamed the streets of Kowloon, seeking adventure wherever they could find it. Bruce, with his excessive energy and fighting prowess, was soon in there with the toughest. He told BLACK BELT magazine in October, 1967, "I was a punk and went looking for fights. We used chains and pens with knives hidden inside them." His family remembers that Bruce kept these weapons in a closet. Bruce often wore a toilet chain wrapped around his waist when he went out on the streets. However, such weapons were, on the whole, more for bravado than anything else. Bruce preferred using his fists. His brothers recall if Bruce didn't like someone, he told him straight to his face, which meant he found plenty of trouble. Fights would start over little or nothing. Dares were the common catalyst. Bruce would run into another youngster in the street and the two would "stare"—he used to tell his brothers and other relatives that nobody had ever "out-stared" him.

When the cast of *Enter the Dragon* traveled to Hong Kong, in the early 1970s, Jim Kelly was surprised at the high crime rate and the toughness of the teenage gangs. He told FIGHTING STARS magazine: "I thought the teenage gangs in the U.S. were tough, but they're real tame compared to those in Hong Kong. The gangs, I think they are called Triads, are vicious."

Bruce explained, "Kids there have nothing to look forward to. The white kids (British) have all the best jobs and the rest of us had to work for them. That's why most of the kids become punks. Life in Hong Kong is so bad. Kids in slums can never get out." Throughout his adult film and television career, Bruce was a big hero to the Hong Kong kids.

Most of the students attending the La Salle College were Chinese Catholics and there was intense rivalry between them and the British schoolchildren attending the King George V School up the hill. The Hong Kong Chinese are not all that fond of the British, an understandable attitude in view of the history of the colony and the relationship based on illusions of racial superiority and inferiority. After school, Bruce and a group of his fellow Chinese students would gather on the hill to taunt the English boys, which inevitably culminated in some rather fierce fighting.

Shortly after he entered La Salle College, Bruce came home one day and told his mother that he wanted to be trained in the martial arts. He said that he was being bullied after school and wanted to learn how to defend himself properly. His father practiced tai chi chuan, which is a series of exercises and moves carried out in slow motion. Bruce had joined his father once or twice doing tai chi but the slowness of the movements did not appeal to Bruce's nature. His mother was sympathetic and agreed to pay the tuition. His teacher was the renowned master Yip Man, an expert in wing chun.

With his introduction to Yip Man, Bruce flung himself into the study of kung fu with frenetic energy. Once his interest was roused in anything, he became a kind of primeval force—his appetite to learn and conquer was voracious. His devotion to kung fu was total. While other students might skip classes, Bruce attended every day after school. The intensity of Bruce's obsession surprised his peers. He seemed to live kung fu. One moment he would be deeply immersed in thought; the next moment he would be on his feet attempting to put into practice the ideas that had been racing through his head. Walking along the street, he would surprise passersby by throwing punches and kicking the leaves off the trees. At home while eating dinner, he would pound away with alternate hands on a stool beside him, to toughen his hands and strengthen his muscles.

Within the first few months of his life Bruce was nicknamed *Mo si tung* (never sits still). From sunup to sundown he was a whirlwind of inquisition. Within time, and out of sheer survival, the family members discovered the only way to keep Bruce quiet was to give him a book to read. And read he did, for hours upon hours.

If there is anything that Yip Man gave to Bruce which may have crystallized Bruce's direction in life, it was to interest his young student in the philosophical teachings of Buddha, Confucius, Lao-Tze, the founders of Taoism and other great Eastern thinkers and spiritual leaders. As a result, Bruce's mind became the distillation of the wisdom of such teachers, specifically, but not exclusively, the deep teachings of the *yin-yang* principle. Yin-yang is generally represented by the double fish symbol, the foundation of which stayed with Bruce and guided him throughout the entirety of his adult life. The following excerpts are reproduced from several English papers Bruce wrote during his college years at the University of Washington:

The *tai chi* (grand terminus) was first drawn more than 3,000 years ago by Chou Chun. The *yang* (whiteness) principle represents positiveness, firmness, maleness, substantiality, brightness, day, heat, etc. The *yin* (blackness) principle is the opposite. It represents negativeness, softness, femaleness, insubstantiality, darkness, night, coldness and so forth.

The basic theory in tai chi is that nothing is so permanent as never to change. In other words, when activity reaches the extreme point, it becomes inactivity, and inactivity forms yin. Extreme inactivity returns to become activity, which is yang. Activity is the cause of inactivity, and vice-versa. This system of complementary increasing and decreasing of the principle is continuous. From this one can see

Bruce's only teacher, Sifu Yip Man, master of the wing chun system of kung fu.

Sifu Yip Man holding baby Brandon, 1965.

Bruce and student, Doug Palmer, practicing chi sao.

that the two forces, although they appear to conflict, in reality are mutually interdependent; instead of opposition, there is cooperation and alternation.

The application of the principles of yin and yang in gung fu* are expressed as the Law of Harmony. It states that one should be in harmony with, not rebellion against, the strength and force of opposition. This means that one should do nothing that is not natural or spontaneous. The important thing is not to strain in any way. When opponent A uses strength (yang) on B, B must not resist him (back) with strength; in other words, do not use positiveness (yang) against positiveness (yang) but instead yield to him with softness (yin) and lead him to the direction of his own force, negativeness (yin) to positiveness (yang). When A's strength goes to the extreme, the positiveness (yang) will change to negativeness (yin), B then taking him at his unguarded moment and attacking with force (yang). Thus the whole process is without being unnatural or strained. B fits his movement harmoniously and continuously into that of A without resisting or striving.

The Law of Harmony gives rise to a closely related law, the law of non-interference with nature, which teaches a gung fu man to forget about himself and follow his opponent (strength) instead of himself; that he does not move ahead but responds to the fitting influence. The basic idea is to defeat the opponent by yielding to him and using his own strength. That is why a gung fu man never asserts himself against his opponent, and never being in frontal opposition to the direction of his force. When being attacked, he will not resist, but will control the attack by swinging with it. This law illustrates the principles of non-resistance and non-violence which were founded on the idea that the branches of a fir tree snapped under the weight of the snow, while the simple reeds, weaker but more supple, can overcome it. Lao-tzu pointed to us the value of gentleness. Contrary to common belief, the yin principle, as softness and pliability, is to be associated with life and survival. Because he can yield, a man can survive. In contrast yang principle which is assumed to be rigorous and hard, makes a man break under pressure.

Editor's Note: Bruce Lee preferred the southern Cantonese pronounciation "gung fu" over the northern Chinese pronounciation of "kung fu." In this book, since "kung fu" has become standardized in English, it is used throughout, except in Bruce's actual writings or the name of his school.

To further illustrate his point, Bruce then quotes some stanzas from Lao-tsu:

Alive, a man is supple, soft;
In death, unbending, rigorous
All creatures, grass and trees, alive
Are plastic but are pliant too
And dead, are friable and dry
Unbending rigor is the mate of death,
And yielding softness, company of life;
Unbending soldiers get no victories;
The stiffest tree is readiest for the ax.
The strong and mighty topple from their place;
The soft and yielding rise above them all.

Bruce continues:

The way of movement in gung fu is closely related to the movement of the mind. In fact, the mind is trained to direct the movement of the body. The mind wills and the body behaves.

To perform the right technique in gung fu, physical loosening must be continued in a mental and spiritual loosening, so as to make the mind not only agile but free. In order to accomplish this, a gung fu man has to remain quiet and calm, and to master the principle of "no mindedness" . . . not a blank mind which excludes all emotion, nor is it simply calmness and quietness of mind. Although quietude and calmness are important, it is the "non-graspiness" of the mind that mainly constitutes the principle of "no-mindedness." A gung fu man employs his mind as a mirror—it grasps nothing, and it refuses nothing; it receives, but does not keep. . . . Let the mind think what it likes without interference by the separate thinker or ego within oneself. So long as it thinks what it wants, there is absolutely no effort in letting it go; and the disappearance of the separate thinker. There is nothing to try to do, for whatever comes up moment by moment is accepted, including non-acceptance . . . It is mind immune to emotional influences . . . No-mindedness is to employ the whole mind as we use the eyes when we rest them upon various objects but make no special effort to take anything in. Therefore, concentration in gung fu does not have the usual sense of restricting the attention to a single sense object, but is simply a quiet awareness of whatever happens to be here and now. Such concentration can be illustrated by an audience at a football game; instead of a concentrated attention on the player who has the ball, he has an awareness of the whole football field. In a similar way, a gung fu man's mind is concentrated by not dwelling on any particular part of the opponent. During sparring, a gung fu man learns to forget about himself and follows the movement of his opponent, leaving his mind free to make its own counter-movement without any interfering deliberation. He frees himself from all mental suggestions of resistance, and adopts a supple attitude. His actions are all performed without self-assertion; he lets his mind remain spontaneous and ungrasped. As soon as he stops to think, his flow of movement will be disturbed and he is immediately struck by his opponent.

In the following years, as fate was to whirl him into unique and demanding environments, Bruce's thinking necessarily became more flexible. He was able to adapt and fit into his changing lifestyle. He wrote:

The world is full of people who are determined to be somebody or give trouble. They want to get ahead, to stand out. Such ambition has no use for a gung fu man, who rejects all forms of self-assertiveness and competition.

A gung fu man, if he is really good, is not proud at all. Pride emphasizes the importance of the superiority of one's status in the eyes of others. There is fear and insecurity in pride because when one aims at being highly esteemed, and having achieved such status, he is automatically involved in the fear of losing his status. Then protection of one's status appears to be his most important need, and this creates anxiety.

Bruce performing the cha-cha. He was the Hong Kong cha-cha champion in 1958.

As we know that gung fu is aiming at self-cultivation and, therefore, the inner self is one's true self; so in order to realize his true self, a gung fu man lives without being dependent upon the opinion of others. Since he is completely self-sufficient he can have no fear of not being esteemed. A gung fu man devotes himself to being self-sufficient, and never depends upon the external rating by others for his happiness. A gung fu master, unlike the beginner, holds himself in reserve, is quiet and unassuming, without the least desire to show off. Under the influence of gung fu training his proficiency becomes spiritual and he himself, grown freer through spiritual struggle, is transformed. To him, fame and status mean nothing.

When he wrote those words, of course, Bruce had no inkling of what the future held in store for him. He had had a slight taste of fame as a child star, but he had little idea of the heights to which he would rise, that he would become a kind of embodiment of all the heroic virtues of the Chinese and other Asian peoples.

By the time he was 15, Bruce was a considerable figure among the kids living in his neighborhood of Kowloon. He was very good-looking and began to take an interest in girls. His brother Peter recalls that Bruce would spend up to 15 minutes in front of the mirror, getting his hair just right, making sure his tie was properly adjusted—a born perfectionist. His looks, self-confidence, and his reputation as a battler, meant that he had little difficulty attracting feminine attention. His attitude toward girls was nicely balanced, too—just the right mixture of self-assurance, sensitivity and easy grace. In short, he brought a formidable array of charms to bear on females who came within his orbit. He even proved to be quite an expert dancer, winning the Crown Colony Cha-Cha Championship in 1958. He kept a list of 108 different steps on a card in his wallet. Whatever Bruce decided to do, whether it was fighting, acting, dancing, or being a friend, he always gave it his all.

Shortly after joining Yip Man's school, Bruce found himself tagging along in the wake of two older boys, Wong Seun-leung and Cheung Cheuk-hing (William Cheung). They were also students of wing chun who, having learned the rudiments of the style, were eager to challenge advocates of the other schools of kung fu. In the main, these were pretty well-conducted and sportsmanlike encounters—young men testing their courage, strength, skills and energies against each other. The two "big brothers" plus Bruce, "the little brother," formed the backbone of the wing chun challengers. To start with, the contests were limited to a handful of participants on either side and were always staged in secret. Eventually, however, the battles became bigger and more open, with rival groups hiring cars and driving out into open spaces in the New Territories. Here judges were selected, rules laid down and a "ring" prepared. These matches continued for a number of years with Bruce and other wing chun

Bruce with his father, Lee Hoi Chuen.

specialists invariably, but not always, coming out on the winning side.

Having been "asked" to leave La Salle College, Bruce moved on to St. Francis Xavier where he was, according to his younger brother Robert, "recognized as the king gorilla—boss of the whole school." It was not so much that Bruce stalked around inflicting physical punishment on less able kids but rather that he never backed down from a challenge. As Robert puts it, "you didn't have to ask Bruce twice to fight."

It was about this time that a great interest was taken in Bruce by an Irish brother at St. Francis Xavier. Brother Kenny had sparred once or twice with Bruce and, realizing just how good he was, encouraged him to enter the interschool boxing championships—boxing, that is, under the Marquis of Queensberry rules. In the interschool finals, Bruce met an English boy from King George V school who had been champion for three years in succession. Bruce adopted his kung fu stance and waited for the other boy, who commenced dancing around in the classic boxing style and then went on the attack, upon which Bruce knocked him out cold!

Trouble, however, was just over the horizon. According to Robert Lee, a challenge was issued to the young men of the Wing Chun School by students of the Choy Li Fut School. Soon the two groups met on the roof of an apartment block in the Resettlement area. Many of these rooftops are laid out as basketball courts and the rule was that whichever school was first to force its opponents over a white line won the contest. The encounter was not meant to be violent, but merely a series of sparring engagements. What began in friendly fashion soon turned ugly when one of the choy li fut boys gave Bruce a black eye. It sent Bruce into an all-out fighting mode and he suddenly unleashed a series of straight punches. He was powerfully fast and the guy couldn't take it. Bruce got him in the face several times and he fell back over the line. Bruce, still in a rage, lashed out with a couple of kicks, catching the guy in the eye and in the mouth and knocking out a tooth.

The boy's parents complained to the police and Mrs. Lee had to go down to the local police station and sign a paper stating that she would take responsibility for Bruce's future good conduct if released in her care. She then took Bruce to a nearby restaurant and had a quiet, yet serious, discussion with him about his future. Mrs. Lee said nothing about the incident to the other members of the family but shortly afterwards suggested to her husband that Bruce, now 18, should exercise his rights and opt for American citizenship. "He hasn't any heart in his studies," she explained to Mr. Lee. All things considered, at that time in his life Bruce never had any hope of gaining admission to college and, had he stayed in Hong Kong, God only knows what might have become of him.

On board the steamship from Hong Kong to the United States in April of 1959, Bruce taught dancing to first-class passengers.

Performing the cha-cha. Bruce wore glasses as a young man which he later traded in for contact lenses.

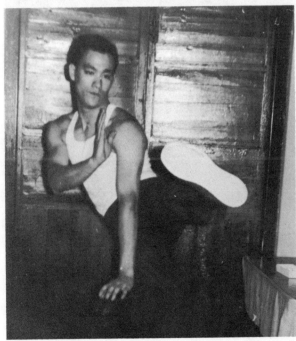

Working out in Hong Kong and playing with a bird in the family home on Nathan Road—summer of 1963.

33

Working out with his father and friends in the Hong Kong countryside.

Bruce arriving home to Hong Kong in 1963. His father on the left is pleased to see his son returning as a successful young man.

And so it was decided that Bruce should return to San Francisco. The steamship he sailed on was one of the American President Lines. The trip took 18 days and was, for Bruce, a time of deep introspection and readjustment. Leaving his family, friends, and the only home he had ever known, for the unknown place of his birth was an exciting as well as anxious experience. Bruce had led a carefree youth, but now he faced an uncertain future not even knowing how he would feed himself after the U.S.$100 he had been given was gone. Reality was descending upon him quickly. But while he contemplated these weighty matters during the trip across the Pacific, Bruce also managed to enjoy himself of course. Although he was booked in second class, he spent most of his time in first class performing demonstrations of the cha-cha and teaching a few of the passengers some of his more intricate steps.

Bruce has been portrayed as a juvenile delinquent, but by and large, I believe this to be an exaggerated picture. Bruce, I'm convinced, was basically much too intelligent not to have realized where to draw the line. When I look at old pictures of my husband, taken when he was at St. Francis Xavier, he looks anything but a rebellious adolescent. The group class pictures show him extremely well dressed in his school blazer, his hair neatly arranged—and, in his glasses, looking every inch the serious and studious young man who inscribed the following earnest entries in his diary:

—November 30, 1958: Now I try to find out my career—whether as a doctor or another? If as a doctor, I must study hard.
—December 1, 1958: Learn more mathematics. Learn more English (conversation).

Bruce's boarding of the trans-Pacific steamship closed a chapter in his life when he had sought to emerge from the teeming millions as a young man with a specific identity and purpose. To have achieved stardom before the age of 18 was hardly the best preparation for building a stable personality. When one adds to this the physical and mental dominance he had established over his contemporaries with his fighting abilities and other skills, I think it remarkable that Bruce managed to come to America as such a well-balanced and even admirable young man.

Practicing a cha-cha move. Bruce had over 100 steps in his repertoire.

In later years, Bruce returned to one of his alma maters, St. Francis Xavier, to present awards.

3

"To me 99 percent of the whole business of Oriental self-defense is baloney. It's fancy jazz. It looks good, but it doesn't work."

—Bruce Lee

Bruce standing in front of his studio on University Way in Seattle. This is the dapper young man I first met in 1963.

Throughout Bruce's life, and even continuing on into the years following his death, there have been a surprising number of martial artists who have attempted to emulate him. Generally speaking, I am not offended by this notion, but rather consider it a compliment to Bruce, both as a martial artist and as a quality human being. What I do find curious, however, is the way in which many of these individuals have gone about trying to achieve their goal by erroneously pursuing the physical aspect and, for the most part, completely ignoring Bruce's incredible mental and spiritual being. There are those who feel they can become like Bruce if they eat what he ate, perform the exact workout schedule he performed, travel to Hong Kong to study wing chun, dress the way he dressed, comb their hair in the exact manner in which he did, and even incorporate his Cantonese accent into their repertoire.

Even more disillusioning are those who have written to me requesting a pair of Bruce's socks or other memorabilia. Several have even offered enormous sums for his 350SL Mercedes, believing that if they drive his car they will take on the very essence of the master. And there have been those who have appeared at Bruce's gravesite in Seattle and proclaimed eternal loyalty and the feeling that they and Bruce "are one." A few have written to tell of personal meetings with Bruce from the "other side." What they neglect is the vitally important reality that the true essence of Bruce's martial arts supremacy centered around a highly trained mental and emotional state.

To illustrate my point, it might perhaps be worth reproducing a series of excerpts from two of many essays Bruce wrote for his freshman English course while attending the University of Washington:

Gung fu is a special skill, a fine art rather than just a physical exercise. It is a subtle art of matching the essence of the mind to that of the technique in which it has to work. The principle of gung fu is not a thing that can be learned, like a science, by fact finding and instruction in facts. It has to grow spontaneously, like a flower, in a mind free from emotion and desires. The core of this principle of gung fu is "Tao"—the spontaneity of the universe.

Bruce further explained that the word *Tao* has no exact equivalent in English, but suggests using the word "truth," and proceeds to explain the truth that every kung fu practitioner should follow:

Tao operates in yin and yang, a pair of mutually complementary forces that are at work in and behind all phenomena. This principle of yin/yang, also known as tai chi, is the basic structure of gung fu.

And as Bruce often vehemently insisted to his students:

Mere technical knowledge of gung fu is not enough to make a man really its master; he ought to have delved deeply into the inner spirit of it. The spirit is grasped only when his mind is in complete harmony with the principle of life itself, that is when he attains to a certain state in Taoism known as "no-mindedness." No-mindedness consists in preserving the absolute fluidity of the mind by keeping it free from intellectual deliberations and effective disturbances of any kind at all. I believe that everybody can think himself into his goal if he mixes his burning desire for its translation into reality.

The following is Bruce's recollection of one of many training experiences with Yip Man:

About four years of hard training in the art of gung fu, I began to understand and felt the principle of gentleness—the art of neutralizing the effect of the opponent's effort and minimizing expenditure of one's energy. All these must be done in calmness and without striving. It sounded simple, but in actual application it was difficult. The moment I engaged in combat with an opponent, my mind was completely perturbed and unstable. Especially after a series of exchanging blows and kicks, all my theory of gentleness was gone. My only one thought left was somehow or another I must beat him and win.

My instructor Professor Yip Man, head of the Wing Chun School, would come up to me and say, "Loong, relax and calm your mind. Forget about yourself and follow the opponent's movement. Let your mind, the basic reality, do the counter-movement without any interfering deliberation. Above all, learn the art of detachment."

That was it! I must relax. However, right there I had already done something contradictory, against my will. That was when I said I must relax, the demand for effort in "must" was already inconsistent with the effortlessness in "relax." When my acute self-consciousness grew to what the psychologists called "double-blind" type, my instructor would again approach me and say, "Loong, preserve yourself by following the natural bends of things and don't interfere. Remember never to assert yourself against nature: never be in frontal opposition to any problem, but control it by swinging with it. Don't practice this week. Go home and think about it."

The following week I stayed home. After spending many hours in

On the steps of Ruby Chow's restaurant where Bruce worked and lived when he first arrived in Seattle—1959.

In the back yard of James Lee's house in Oakland.

37

meditation and practice, I gave up and went sailing alone in a junk. On the sea, I thought of all my past training and got mad at myself and punched at the water. Right then at that moment, a thought suddenly struck me. Wasn't this water, the very basic stuff, the essence of gung fu? Didn't the common water just illustrate to me the principle of gung fu? I struck it just now, but it did not suffer hurt. Again I stabbed it with all my might, yet it was not wounded. I then tried to grasp a handful of it but it was impossible. This water, the softest substance in the world, could fit into any container. Although it seemed weak, it could penetrate the hardest substance in the world. That was it! I wanted to be like the nature of water.

Suddenly a bird flew past and cast its reflection on the water. Right then, as I was absorbing myself, another mystic sense of hidden meaning started upon me. Shouldn't it be the same then that the thoughts and emotions I had in front of an opponent passed like the reflection of the bird over the water? This was exactly what Professor Yip Man meant by being detached—not being without emotion or feeling, but being one in whom feeling was not sticky or blocked. Therefore, in order to control myself I must first accept myself by going with, and not against, my nature. I lay on the boat and felt that I had united with Tao; I had become one with nature. I just lay there and let the boat drift freely and irresistibly according to its own will. For at that moment I had achieved a state of inner feeling in which opposition had become mutually cooperative instead of mutually exclusive, in which there was no longer any conflict in my mind. The whole world to me was unitary.

Bruce in a typical wing chun stance.

This was the way Bruce's mind worked at age 18 or 20. In essence, Professor Yip Man guided Bruce to the spiritual aspect of kung fu, an aspect which back in the late 1950s was, and still is, for the most part omitted by martial arts instructors teaching in the United States. The spiritual side of the martial arts is not commercially salable in the Western world. Students who take up the martial arts in the U.S. are primarily interested in learning physical movement, some for health reasons, others for self-defense, and still others because they intend to pursue tournament competition. Very few beginning martial arts students are all that interested in the spiritual and philosophical concepts of the Far East. One might imagine the expression on the face of the beginning student whose instructor tells him or her to go home for a week and "think about no-mindedness."

One must remember also that the religious backbone of the Western world is Christianity. As a result, parents of children bent on studying the art have frequently been known to approach potential instructors wanting to know whether or not their child is going to be subjected to Buddhist principles or Zen meditation. From a legal standpoint, especially in light of the fact that in today's Western world malicious lawsuits are a commonplace reality, even those few instructors who may be capable of teaching those principles taught years ago to Bruce are highly reluctant to do so if there be any suspicion that they would be guiding some

Bruce and Taky Kimura working on a throwing technique.

Bruce practicing high kicks, a rarity except for show. Note how he traced lines and arrows on his photos to study the techniques. His flexibility was superb.

child, or even adult, down some path which could be interpreted as contrary to their religious beliefs. In sharp contrast, not only was Bruce attracted to the spiritual aspect of the martial art, he pursued it with great fervor. In the final analysis, it was the single element, even above and beyond his physical prowess and expertise, which made him incredibly unique, and subsequently highly sought after.

If there is any single question regarding Bruce's life as a martial artist which has baffled so many other martial artists it is this: How could a young man in his early 20s, having studied a relatively simple style of kung fu for a mere five years (wing chun is a simple style founded by a frail nun, and for the most part is without kicks and has only three simple forms), a man who weighed less than 150 pounds and stood just over five-foot-seven—how could this individual have stood in front of the entire martial arts community in the United States and said that over 95 percent of all that he saw and heard was utter nonsense—let alone make it stick?! Quite obviously Bruce had something of great importance, something exclusively unique to him, the very essence of which was far more than simply an expert knowledge of the physical movements of wing chun. Although Bruce was only 18 years of age when he arrived in San Francisco from Hong Kong, he brought with him a profound inner knowledge of both himself and the world in which he moved and breathed.

In the early months, life in the States proved no tougher nor easier than it had been for millions of immigrants before him. Indeed, upon his arrival Bruce was already a citizen and possessed a rudimentary grasp of English, although he had to work hard to improve it. He found shelter and work among the various Chinese communities. He first stayed with an old friend of his father's in San Francisco and earned a little money giving dance lessons. Then Ruby Chow, a Seattle restaurant owner and important figure in local politics, offered him a room above her restaurant as a gesture of friendship to his father and in return for his services as a waiter. Bruce jumped at the chance of a steady job and moved to Seattle. He attended Edison Technical School during the day to earn his high school diploma, and at night worked in Ruby Chow's, often doubling with a job as a newspaper "stuffer" (inserting loose advertisements or give-away announcements inside the printed pages) of the *Seattle Times*.

One of Bruce's first friends in Seattle was Taky Kimura. Taky is a Japanese-American businessman who was 38 years old at the time he met Bruce. Taky had been interned during the Second World War and as a consequence, he had difficulty finding a job in the post-war era with its prevailing anti-Japanese sentiment. He had lost a great deal of self-confidence and had taken to the martial arts in the hope of restoring some of it. "I was taking judo about 1959," explains Taky. "I got hurt two or three times by

Bruce kidding around at James Lee's house.

Bruce and Taky Kimura.

41

In his childhood home at 218 Nathan Road, Kowloon, Hong Kong, Bruce poses in a typical martial arts posture wearing pajama bottoms.

some people who offered me nothing but brawn. I was really getting demoralized by that time. Some of the people who went to one of Bruce's classes came by the supermarket where I was working. They told me how they met this amazing young man from Hong Kong. Of course, I thought to myself, I've seen a little bit of everything and it can't be that much. But they kept on telling me that he was 'incredible.' At that time, these fellows were practicing out in the backyards and in city parks. So I went out to the university area to the football field, and that's when I first met him. I was so amazed and impressed with his ability that I immediately asked him if I could join his club and for almost a year we just met at parks on Sundays. I was intrigued by his tremendous power, of being light one minute and really deep the next.''

Taky and Bruce became lifelong friends from that time on, and Taky became very skilled in the Jun Fan kung fu that Bruce was teaching then. In fact when Bruce left Seattle years later, Taky became his first assistant instructor, a title he retains to this day.

But even in those early days of teaching in backyards and city parks, Bruce was formulating grander plans. He was determined to succeed as can be seen from his writings some 14 years later:

> Ever since I was a child I have had this instinctive urge for expansion and growth. To me, the function and duty of a quality human is the sincere and honest development of one's potential. I have come to discover through earnest personal experience and dedicated learning that ultimately the greatest help is self-help; that there is no other help but self-help—doing one's best, dedicating one's self wholeheartedly to a given task, which happens to have no end but is an on-going process. I have done a lot during these years of my process, I have changed from blindly following propaganda, organized truths, etc., to search internally for the cause of my ignorance.

As a footnote I feel it important to mention that throughout Bruce's adult life he was an avid reader of the great authors of the concept of ''self help,'' including Norman Vincent Peale, Napolean Hill, W. Clement Stone, Gyula Denes, and Dr. Maxwell Maltz, to name only a few.

At Edison, Bruce began in earnest that long battle to understand himself and his art which, as he himself stated, ''happens to have no end.'' He forced himself to work hard at math and science, the areas in which he was most ignorant, although managing to enjoy himself in history and philosophy. In gaining his high school diploma, he secured satisfactory grades and was admitted to the University of Washington—something which his family would have considered an unlikely feat only two years earlier. He was a determined and dynamic young man, confident of his own abilities and, who, like all outstanding personalities not inclined to follow the crowd, clashed frequently with other strong-willed individuals.

As his friend Jhoon Rhee, grandmaster of tae kwon do, has said, ''Bruce generally tended to be direct and straightforward in his remarks, particularly when talking about the martial arts. In his almost desperate attempts to explain himself and his ideas without ambiguity, he often found himself clashing with exponents of classical kung fu, karate and other forms." Later, in 1967, Bruce summed up his ideas tersely but unequivocally to BLACK BELT magazine. He insisted that kung fu had to rest on "realism and plausibility" and argued that it was difficult to find worthwhile instruction in the art.

"There's too much horsing around with unrealistic stances and classic forms and rituals," he explained. "It's just too artificial and mechanical and doesn't really prepare a student for actual combat. A guy could be clobbered while getting into his classical mess. Classical methods like these, which I consider a form of paralysis, only solidify and condition what was once fluid. These practitioners are merely blindly rehearsing systematic routines and stunts that will lead to nowhere."

He described this type of teaching as little more than "organized despair" and, commenting on classical versions of kung fu, emphasized the virtues of simplicity and directness. "To me 99 percent of the whole business of Oriental self-defense is baloney," he declared to reporters. "It's fancy jazz. It looks good, but it doesn't work. If a 90-pound woman is attacked by a 250-pound man, the only thing she can do is strike hard at one of three places—the eyeballs, the groin or the shins. This should be sufficient to put the man off balance for just a moment and then she'd better run like hell.

"Or this matter of breaking bricks and boards with the edge of your hand," he continued. "How often, I ask you, did you ever see a brick or a board pick a fight with anybody? This is gimmick stuff. A human being doesn't just stand there and wait to be hit. So many karate students are wrapped up in the snorting sounds and the countermoves that they lose sight of what they should be doing to an opponent—getting him out of there, quick. The karate teacher says, 'If your opponent does this, then you do this, and then you do this and then you do this.' And while you are remembering the 'and-thens,' the other guy is killing you. Faced with the choice of hitting your opponent in the ribs or poking him in the eyes, you go for the eyes every time."

Bruce, I must emphasize, never deliberately set out to make enemies, but it was perhaps inevitable that he should rub some people the wrong way. In his sheer enthusiasm for kung fu, he often appeared cocky. He could not conceal his zeal for a reformation of the traditional attitudes.

For example, he came to scoff at the idea of a separation between the "hard" and "soft" schools of kung fu. "It's an illusion," he declared. "You see, in reality gentleness/firmness is one inseparable force of one unceasing interplay of movement. We hear a lot of teachers claiming that their styles are the soft and

Bruce demonstrates his musculature and feats of strength.

Note the dotted lines and arrows Bruce drew to dissect his movements.

others claiming that theirs are the hard; these people are clinging blindly to one partial view of the totality. I was once asked by a so-called Chinese kung fu 'master'—one of those that really looked the part with beard and all—as to what I thought of *yin* (soft) and *yang* (firm)? I simply answered 'baloney!' Of course, he was quite shocked at my answer and could not come to the realization that 'it' is never two.''

Bruce eventually came to christen his own teaching *jeet kune do* (the way of the intercepting fist); yet, he resolutely insisted that it ought never to be described as a "style." He thought the words inaccurate in relation to what he was trying to do and once explained, "Fundamentally all styles claim their methods as being able to cope with 'all' types of attacks. In other words, their structure covers all possible lines and angles as well as being capable of retaliating from all angles and lines. Since all possible lines and angles are covered, whence comes all these 'different' styles?

"I guess he who claims his style is really different must assume his stance on his head and when he strikes, he must turn and spin three times before doing so. After all, how many ways are there to come in on an opponent without deviating from the natural and direct path? By 'different,' probably these instructors go only for straight lines, or maybe just round lines, or maybe only kicking or maybe even just looking different, flapping here and flicking there. To me, styles that cling to one partial aspect of combat are actually in bondage. You see, a chosen method, however exacting, fixes its practitioners in an enclosed pattern. I always say that actual combat is never fixed, has no boundaries or limits, and is constantly changing from moment to moment. All of a sudden, the opponent is 'alive' and no longer a cooperative robot. In other words, once 'conditioned' in the partialized style, its practitioner faces his opponent through a screen of resistance. In reality, he is merely 'performing' his stylized blocks and listening to his own screams.''

To further aggravate matters, Bruce used to poke fun at many martial arts instructors. "Of all the athletes in the world, only in the martial arts do they come so fat and in poor condition. And you know what? They're usually the instructors. Yep, only in the martial arts can the instructor can get away with it. Because he can bluff his way with his mouth. He doesn't have to prove himself—he doesn't have to spar. He just has to convince his students that he's indestructible and who's going to challenge him? These guys are all too ritualistic, what with their bowing and posturing. That sort of Oriental self-defense is like swimming on land. You can learn all the swimming strokes, but if you're never in the water, it's meaningless. These guys never fight. They all want to break three-inch boards or two bricks or something. Why? That doesn't make them fighters.''

Such statements were controversial enough, and it's perhaps

Bruce doing his one-hand, two-finger push-ups.

useless to deny that many martial arts instructors were highly annoyed with Bruce, although the very best of them, such as Jhoon Rhee and Ed Parker, however much they disagreed with Bruce, respected him for his honest views and integrity and became his lifelong friends.

In the early years, however, there were those who had to be shown. A Japanese karate black belt attending one of Bruce's early demonstrations in Seattle objected to opinions and ideas expressed along similar lines and challenged Bruce. Bruce tried to explain that he intended nothing personal and that he was not attempting to downgrade anyone but merely explaining the essence of his own methods. The karate expert repeated his challenge and Bruce was forced to accept. The two repaired to a nearby gym, followed by a large, excited crowd. The fight was short and spectacular. The karate man opened up with a kick which Bruce, still using the wing chun method, blocked. Using his straight punches, typical wing chun, Bruce drove the black belt back toward the white line and then knocked him across it, finishing him off with a kick to the face. The karate expert was so impressed that he became one of Bruce's avid followers. As Bob Wall, the West Coast karate instructor once said, "The only thing I hate about Bruce is he can do anything he says." To which Taky Kimura added, "A lot of people took exception, but when they saw what he could do, they all wanted to join him."

Bruce had been sorely tempted shortly after his arrival in the United States from Hong Kong in April, 1959, to open a *kwoon* (training hall) in San Francisco and go into teaching. He told BLACK BELT magazine that several karatemen he had met during his first six months there "wanted me to start a *dojo* (kwoon) in San Francisco but I wasn't interested. I wanted to further my education."

In sharp contrast, however, he also recalled that he disliked the odd jobs he had to do to support himself when he first came to Seattle and added, half-jokingly, "I was too lazy for that kind of routine and began teaching kung fu on the side." The fact is Bruce could no more abandon kung fu, even temporarily, than he could stop breathing. As for being lazy . . . selectively lazy, I would say.

Bruce never really consciously set out to achieve the worldwide fame which, in fact, eventually came his way. This does not mean that he was not conscious of the need to earn a livelihood, nor that he did not dream of making the world more conscious of his beloved kung fu. In a letter written to an old friend in Hong Kong in September, 1962, long before he had broken into acting in Hollywood, Bruce reveals not only his ambitions for the future but his determination to make the art of kung fu more widely known:

> This letter is hard to understand. It contains my dreams and my ways of thinking. As a whole, you can call it my way of life. It will be

Finding space to practice in Hong Kong was difficult. Note the resettlement housing in the background.

One-hand, three-finger push-ups. Bruce's upper body was well-developed from this type of exercise.

Bruce's class at St. Francis Xavier School in Hong Kong. Bruce is in the second row, third from the left.

Grandmaster Jhoon Rhee introducing Bruce at his tournament in Washington, D.C.

Bruce practicing with family friend, Sylvia Lai, a popular Hong Kong entertainer who would later be Robert Lee's wife.

rather confusing as it is difficult to write down exactly how I feel. Yet, I want to write and let you know about it. I'll do my best to write it clearly and I hope that you, too, will keep an open mind in this letter, and don't arrive at any conclusions till you are finished.

There are two ways of making a good living. One is the result of hard work, and the other, the result of the imagination (requires work, too, of course). It is a fact that labor and thrift produce a competence, but fortune, in the sense of wealth, is the reward of the man who can think of something that hasn't been thought of before. In every industry, in every profession, ideas are what America is looking for. Ideas have made America what she is, and one good idea will make a man what he wants to be.

One part of my life is gung fu. This art influences greatly in the formation of my character and ideas. I practice gung fu as a physical culture, a form of mental training, a method of self-defense, and a way of life. Gung fu is the best of all martial art; yet the Chinese derivatives of judo and karate, which are only basics of gung fu, are flourishing all over the U.S. This so happens because no one has heard of this supreme art, also there are no competent instructors. I believe my long years of practice back up my title to become the first instructor of this movement. There are yet long years ahead of me to polish my techniques and character. My aim, therefore, is to establish a first gung fu institute that will later spread out all over the U.S. (I have set a time limit of 10-15 years to complete the whole project.) My reason in doing this is not the sole objective of making money. The motives are many and among them are: I like to let the world know about the greatness of this Chinese art; I enjoy teaching and helping people; I like to have a well-to-do home for my family; I like to originate something; and the last but yet one of the most important is because gung fu is part of myself.

I know my idea is right, and therefore, the results would be satisfactory. I don't really worry about the reward, but to set in motion the machinery to achieve it. My contribution will be the measure of my reward and success.

Before he passed away, some asked the late Dr. Charles P. Steinmetz, the electrical genius, in his opinion "What branch of science would make the most progress in the next 25 years?" He paused and thought for several minutes, then, like a flash, replied, "Spiritual realization." When man comes to a conscious vital realization of those great spiritual forces within himself and begins to use those forces in science, in business, and in life, his progress in the future will be unparalleled.

When you drop a pebble into a pond of water, the pebble starts a series of ripples that extend until they encompass the whole pool. This is exactly what will happen when I give my ideas a definite plan of action. Right now I can project my thoughts into the future. I can see ahead of me. I dream (remember that practical dreamers never quit). I may now own nothing but a little place down in a basement, but once my imagination has got up a full head of steam, I can see, painted on a canvas in my mind, a picture of a fine, big five- or six-story gung fu institute with branches all over the States. I am not easily discouraged, and I readily visualize myself as overcoming obstacles, winning out over setbacks, achieving "impossible" objectives.

Bruce then relates the old Hindu legend where the Supreme Being decided to implant the "God-head" inside man himself "because man will never think to look for it within himself." He continued:

> Whether it is the God-head or not, I feel this great force, this untapped power, this dynamic something with me. This feeling defies description, and no experience with which this feeling may be compared. It is something like a strong emotion mixed with faith, but a lot stronger.

> All in all, the goal of my planning and doing is to find the true meaning in life—peace of mind. I know that the sum of all the possessions I mentioned does not necessarily add up to peace of mind; however, it can be if I devote to real accomplishment of self rather than neurotic combat. In order to achieve this peace of mind, the teaching of detachment of Taoism and Zen proved to be valuable.

> Probably, people will say I'm too conscious of success. Well, I am not. You see, my will to do springs from the knowledge that *I can do*. I'm only being natural, for there is no fear or doubt inside my mind. Success comes to those who are success-conscious. If you don't aim at the object, how the heck on earth do you think you can get it?"

When he wrote these foregoing passages, Bruce was only in his early 20s and had been in the U.S. just three or four years. His command of the English language was outstanding, better than many native-born Americans and incredible for someone who did not even start learning the language until he was 12 years old. I had not yet met Bruce at this time, but when I did just a year later, he had a clear idea of the kind of future he wanted, how he was going to achieve it, and how to reconcile his ambitions and dreams and whatever success came his way with the underlying principles of kung fu.

By late 1963, Bruce had issued a prospectus for his kung fu institute, which was installed on University Way near the college campus in Seattle. The regular fee was $22 per month and $17 for juniors. The prospectus, which was printed and illustrated, warned that kung fu could *not* be mastered in three easy lessons. Intelligent thinking and hard work were required. Emphasizing the simplicity of the art, Bruce promised that "techniques are smooth, short, and extremely fast; they are direct, to the point and are stripped down to their essential purpose without any wasted motions." He promised that kung fu would develop confidence, humility, coordination, adaptability and respect for others.

And so it began. Less than a year later, Bruce and I were married and were on our way to Oakland. Ahead lay an exciting period of struggle, of hard work and frustration, phases of high euphoria and moments of near-despair and despondency. There

Bruce at the age of 23 when I first met him in 1963.

were times when we were not to have a lot of money, times when it seemed that success was just around the corner. In many ways it was an unsettling life—we moved from house to house no fewer than 11 times in our nine-year marriage. Yet, we were never really hard up and just being with Bruce was more than enough for me. We had our years of struggle, but it was a welcome struggle. Bruce had goals, ambitions and achievements to be realized and knew that for these to become realities he had to put as much into life as he expected to gain from it.

4

Our first home together was in James Lee's house in Oakland, California. Shortly after we moved in, James' wife died suddenly, leaving him with two young children. James, Karena, Greglon, Bruce and I became one family, and Brandon would soon make us six. Over the years I have occasionally read articles in assorted magazines which have exaggerated our poverty at this time. In fact, the Jun Fan Gung Fu Institute which Bruce and James established on Broadway initially proved quite successful. The few hundred dollars per month that the institute cleared were sufficient to cover our expenses.

Several months after Bruce and James had begun teaching, a kung fu practitioner from San Francisco issued a challenge to Bruce. He had recently arrived in the United States from Hong Kong and was seeking to establish himself as a leading *sifu* (teacher) in the Chinatown community. There are interesting historical reasons which formed the basis of this challenge which I feel will set the stage for what ensued.

In the early 1900s, Chinese immigrants to California and other Western states were often the subjects of merciless discrimination by Caucasians who saw these gentle, hard-working pigtailed people as the advanced guard of "The Yellow Peril"—and, even more to the point, a source of cheap labor. From the 1870s onward, China itself had been subject to increasing foreign exploitation, particularly by the British. Because of this, secret societies practicing kung fu and other martial arts were formed to help eject the "foreign devils" from the ancient land. Pupils were led to believe that those who had mastered kung fu could overcome anything and a kind of holy frenzy took hold of young men who believed that they could defeat foreign bombs and bullets with only their bare fists. Some instructors even fired blanks to

Ed Parker's first impression had been that Bruce was cocky but he decided, after seeing Bruce in action, that he "had every right to be—he could make the air pop when he hit."

James Lee's house in Oakland was Bruce's and my first home.

James Y. Lee. James passed away in December, 1972.

"prove" to their pupils that bullets could not hurt them. It was in this spirit then, that at the beginning of this century thousands of young Chinese attacked the British and American armies in the uprising known as the Boxer Rebellion. The Chinese were slaughtered by the thousands.

With this historical attitude in mind, it is not surprising that in the early 1960s, Chinese, particularly in America, were reluctant to disclose the secrets of their martial arts to Caucasians. It became an unwritten law that the art should be taught only to Chinese. Bruce considered such thinking completely outmoded. When it was argued that white men, if taught the secrets, would use the art to injure Chinese, Bruce pointed out that if a white man really wanted to hurt a Chinese, there were plenty of other ways he could do it. "After all, he's bigger."

However, Bruce soon found that at first his views were not shared by some members of the Chinese community in San Francisco, particularly those in martial arts circles. One of these was the challenger who, on the date of the appointed challenge, appeared at Bruce's kwoon on Broadway, accompanied by several Chinese colleagues. He handed Bruce an ornate scroll in Chinese, formally announcing the challenge. Bruce read the scroll which appeared to have been an ultimatum from the San Francisco martial arts community. It stated that if Bruce lost the challenge, he was to either close down his institute or stop teaching Caucasians. Bruce looked at the man.

"Is this what you want?"

The challenger seemed almost apologetic. "Well, no, this is not what I want—but I'm representing these people here." He indicated his Chinese comrades.

"Okay, then," said Bruce.

This had an extraordinary effect on the kung fu man and his supporters (another half-dozen or so of his pupils had now drifted in). Obviously they had imagined that Bruce was a paper tiger who, faced with an actual challenge by a skilled practitioner, would simply chicken out. They went into what I can only describe as a huddle. When it broke up, they suggested to Bruce, "Let's not make this a match—let's just spar together. Let's just try out our techniques."

Bruce swept this aside impatiently and angrily. Few men had a quicker temper.

"No, you challenged me. So let's fight!" An all-out fight was obviously the last thing these guys had envisioned, even though they had been the ones to issue the challenge in the first place. Their next move was to try and negotiate some rules so that no one would get seriously hurt.

"No hitting in the face. No kicking in the groin," began the challenger.

"I'm not standing for any of that!" declared Bruce. "You've

come here with an ultimatum and a challenge, hoping to scare me off. You've made the challenge—so I'm making the rules. So, as far as I'm concerned, it's no-holds-barred. It's all out!''

At that moment, I was over eight months pregnant with our son Brandon. I suppose I ought to have been nervous. Yet, the truth is that I felt quite calm and composed under the circumstances. I knew Bruce was angered and hot-tempered, but he appeared to be in perfect control of his physical and emotional being. I had no doubt that he could take care of himself.

Bruce and the alleged expert bowed formally and then began to fight. Bruce's opponent adopted a classic stance whereas Bruce, who at the time was still using his wing chun style, produced a series of straight punches. Within one minute, the men who had accompanied the challenger were trying to stop the fight as Bruce began to achieve the upper hand. James Lee warned them to let the fight go on. A minute later, with Bruce continuing the attack in earnest, his opponent began to backpedal as fast as he could. For an instant, the fight threatened to degenerate into a farce as he actually turned and ran. When the two men returned to the center of the gym, Bruce's opponent was unable to mount an attack. Bruce quickly brought him to the floor and poised above him with his fist raised.

"Is that enough?" shouted Bruce.

"That's enough!" pleaded his adversary. Bruce demanded a second reply to his question to make sure that he understood that this was the end of the fight.

Still highly incensed, Bruce dragged the man to his feet and then threw the whole bunch off the premises. I don't think I've ever seen a more startled group of kung fu fighters before or since, and from that point forward the San Francisco martial arts community never again dared to threaten Bruce directly. As Al Dacascos put it years later, "And that was the last time Bruce had any trouble with the Chinese community. In fact, if you go down into San Francisco's Chinatown today—or any other Chinatown —you'll find that Bruce is the great hero. They'll tell you, 'Yeah, Bruce is a Chinaman and he's a great kung fu man!' and they couldn't be more proud of him.''

Bruce's whole life was an evolving process, and this has never been seen to greater effect than in his work with the martial arts. The clash I have just described with the kung fu challenger from San Francisco caused Bruce to question his own personal expression of martial arts. Until this battle, he had largely been content to improvise and expand on his original wing chun style but then he suddenly realized that although he had won with comparative ease, his performance had been neither crisp nor efficient. The fight, he realized, ought to have ended within a few seconds of him striking the first blow. Instead, it had dragged on for three minutes. In addition, at its conclusion Bruce had felt unusually

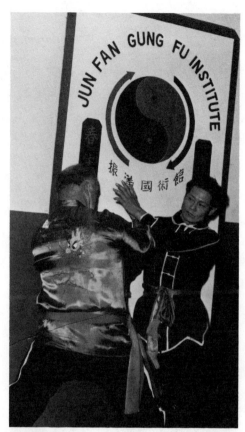

James Lee at the Jun Fan Gung Fu Institute in Oakland.

James Lee doing his famous brick-breaking technique.

This is me pregnant with Brandon.

Bruce holding his newborn daughter, Shannon.

winded, which proved to him that he was in a far from perfect physical condition. So he began to dissect the fight, seeking to find ways where he could have improved his performance. Ultimately he concluded that the basis of wing chun was restrictive for him. It placed too much importance on hand techniques, had very few kicking techniques and therefore was, essentially, partial. Once he realized the physical limitations of the wing chun style, he began to branch out, to explore, to test new movements, to rethink the traditional styles. He did not do this by jumping about from style to style or instructor to instructor, but rather by searching inwardly for the best within himself, rejecting the unsuitable and retaining the appropriate. He may have found this easier than most people because he had always felt a personal obligation to himself to be the best at whatever he did—not the biggest or most successful—but rather to express himself to the highest degree of which he was capable.

That fight also caused Bruce to pursue more sophisticated and exhaustive training methods. Gradually, he came to develop several pieces of equipment that he felt would be of great help. I often saw him sit down and draw ideas for special equipment on a piece of paper. Usually his friend and student, Herb Jackson, an expert and innovative craftsman, would build the apparatus. Bruce constantly sought more realistic equipment. Heavy bags and dummies, after all, cannot fight back. So he tried to develop equipment that would increase reaction speed—equipment that would come back at him from different angles, forcing him to change, to move, to be aware, and most of all to remain active. But even the best equipment cannot simulate real combat conditions. For this reason the main element of his training was to spar, and throughout his life he did as much unrehearsed sparring as possible.

"To me the best exercise is running," Bruce once told a reporter, emphasizing that "nobody who was not thoroughly fit had any business doing any hard sparring." He insisted that "running is so important that you should keep it up during your lifetime. What time of the day is not important so long as you run. In the beginning you should jog easily and then gradually increase the distance and tempo, and finally include sprinting to develop your wind." He himself ran daily for between 15 and 45 minutes, covering from two to six miles. In addition, he covered 10-20 miles every second day on his stationary bicycle and often went for bicycle rides with Brandon. Besides running, he also strongly believed in exercises for the abdomen—sit-ups, leg raises and so forth. "Too often one of those big-belly Chinese masters will tell you that his *chi* (internal power) has sunk to his stomach. He's not kidding, it has sunk—and gone!"

Bruce believed his punches and kicks had to be sharpened and improved daily to be efficient. One unique piece of equipment

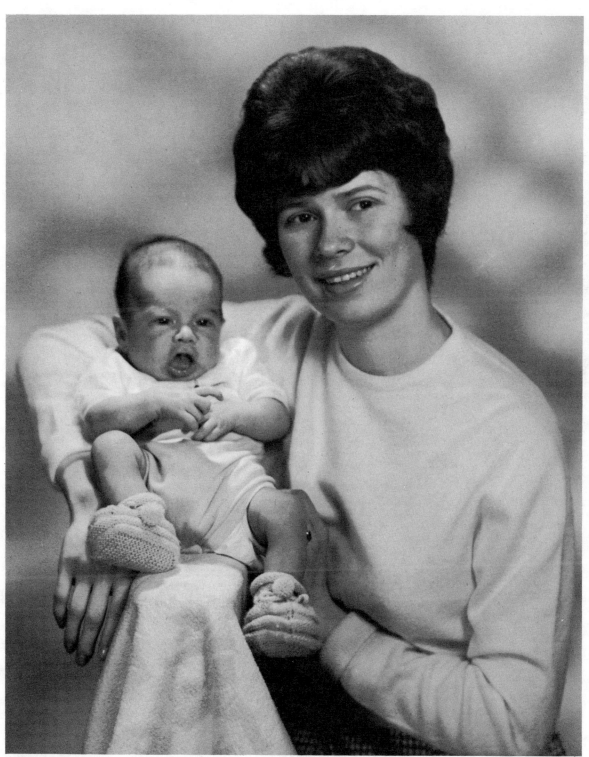

Brandon and I. Note the head of jet-black hair he was born with, soon to turn blond.

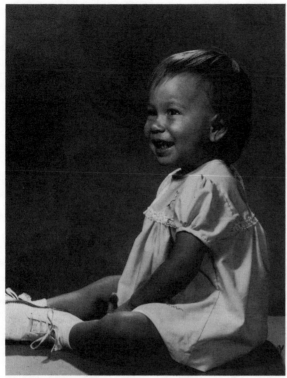

Baby Shannon, the apple of her daddy's eye.

Brandon about two years old practicing his moves.

Our family posing for a publicity photo in the Kato years.

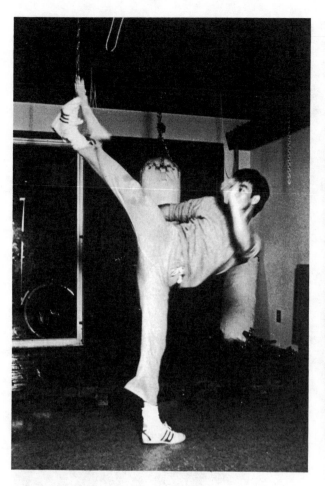

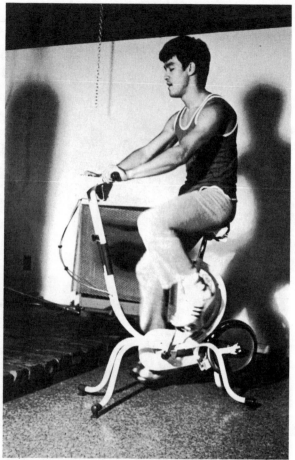

Bruce using a hanging paper target, on the exercise bike, and working out with the wooden dummy.

Wearing a traditional "gung fu" uniform, Bruce practiced wing chun techniques on the wooden dummy.

Bruce and Dan Inosanto, his senior student and assistant instructor of the Jun Fan Gung Fu Institute in Los Angeles.

was a wing chun wooden dummy which he originally had brought over from Hong Kong. He made it increasingly sophisticated as he progressed within his art. This piece of equipment was about six feet high and a foot in diameter. It stood on an eight-by-eight-foot platform and was supported by springy metal, which meant that its reaction to a punch was fairly unpredictable. It had two portable hands below the neck and another in the center which stretched out about two feet. The dummy also had a metal leg which extended out and down. The hands helped in practicing for example *pak sao* (a trapping technique) and also for techniques in *chi sao* (sticking hands). The importance of the dummy's leg was that it taught the martial artist to place his foot in such a way as to automatically lock his opponent's front leg, thus preventing him from kicking or scooping. Moreover, a student could also practice shin kicks on the dummy.

Bruce, in fact, used several different punching bags. In addition to a punching bag filled with beans attached to a wall, a heavy bag was used for unleashing heavy, continuous punches designed to keep an opponent off balance. He also used a "top-and-bottom" bag to hit straight. "If you don't hit it straight, the bag will not return to you," he explained. It was useful in developing footwork. Supported by elastic cords on the top and the bottom, the bag always returned with enormous speed so that the practitioner had to remain on constant alert. He used a round focus pad with an assistant holding it to simulate a moving target. The importance of this was that it taught him not to telegraph his punches. It looked something like a catcher's mitt, except that it was flat. Bruce used to carry one of these things around with him and if he met anyone interested in the martial arts he would put it on and say "Here, take a swing—all you've got." Most people would first wind up and then hit it. Bruce would ask them to put it on, then demonstrate that it was not necessary to wind up to deliver a punch—all anyone needed was a short distance. The severity of the resulting blow was such that, on one occasion, he actually dislocated the shoulder of a man in the offices of BLACK BELT magazine.

He even utilized ordinary paper in his workouts. He would hang a sheet of paper on a heavy rope or chain at a chosen height. The purpose of this was to help increase speed and to ensure the correct application of the body for power. It helped develop his hip movement in punching and was also useful for both side and hook kicking. Aside from teaching him to judge distance, its essential purpose was to encourage precision and crisp movement.

Easily one of his most spectacular training movements involved the use of an air shield. This was fascinating to watch. If Bruce held the target for a student, I never saw the student's kick shake him. However, when it came to Bruce's turn to deliver the kick, the pupil often ended up across the room flat on his back.

When Bruce's younger brother Robert came to live with us from Hong Kong, he remembers that however hard he tried to brace himself to take one of Bruce's kicks at the air shield, he inevitably ended up in the rear garden—but as he adds, "fortunately Linda always opened the door first." The shield was also used to improve penetration. If a partner or pupil thought that Bruce intended to attack, he could try to back away as quickly as possible, though such were Bruce's penetrative powers that even top karatemen found themselves unable to evade him during workouts.

Bruce constantly emphasized that the best training of all was free-style sparring using protective equipment. "In sparring you should wear suitable protective equipment and go all out. Then you can truly learn the correct timing and distance for the delivery of kicks, punches, and so forth. It's a good idea to spar with all types of individuals—tall, short, fast, clumsy—yes, at times a clumsy fellow will mess up a better man because his awkwardness serves as a sort of broken rhythm. The best sparring partner, though, is a quick, strong man who does not know anything, a madman who goes all out scratching, grabbing, punching, kicking."

This then was Bruce's life in the 60s. Up early every day followed by a warm-up of stretching and perhaps a run before breakfast or an hour on his stationary bicycle. The he relaxed by reading, watching some TV, playing with the kids (Brandon was joined by our daughter Shannon in 1969) or making business calls. An early lunch was followed by more heavy reading and a rigorous workout. Then before turning in around 11:00 p.m., he would dictate to his cassette tape recorder all the matters he needed to attend to the following day. In keeping with his childhood nickname, throughout each and every day Bruce was rarely still. He was the nearest thing to perpetual motion in a human as is possible to imagine.

5

"Bruce was one in two billion."
—Ed Parker

Bruce with life-long friend and "second mother," Eva Tso.

The institute in Oakland was not doing as well as either Bruce or James Lee had originally hoped. There was only one real reason for this—Bruce was a perfectionist who was determined to admit only serious pupils whom he felt were worth spending time on. Bruce once told a reporter in an interview, "Sincere and serious learners are equally difficult to come by. Many of them are five-minute enthusiasts, some of them come with ill intention, but unfortunately, most of them are secondhand artists, basically conformers." Moreover, Bruce made a point of the exclusivity of his kwoon—that it was limited to honored members only, that it was the only one of its kind in the world, that all lessons were personalized, and so on. He listed the motives for taking lessons in kung fu—for good health, for self-defense, for securing the admiration of others, self-improvement and, above all, peace of mind.

When we moved to Los Angeles in 1966, Bruce opened his third kwoon in Chinatown at 628 College Street. Danny Inosanto, who became his assistant instructor, says, "Bruce never liked to commercialize his art, so he just painted the windows red. He didn't like signs outside the door and that sort of thing." What struck Danny most about Bruce as an instructor was how totally relaxed he was, constantly making jokes and keeping everyone in good humor, yet at the same time, "maintaining proper discipline."

In sharp contrast, Danny recalls his initial introduction to Bruce as a teacher, "The secret of kicking, as Bruce taught it, was controlled anger. I remember once he asked me to try kicking. He held this shield and for five minutes, I kicked at that shield, desperately trying to improve my kick. I really thought I was giving it my all—but Bruce still wasn't satisfied. Finally, he came over and slapped me on the face—at the same time calling out, 'Now kick!' He held up the shield—I was simply blazing with anger and went pow! It was fantastic.'' Bruce rarely used this type of incentive in teaching, but he knew Dan's temperament well enough to know it was necessary.

Danny says, ''The result was that training with Bruce was far more than just learning a way of fighting or of defending yourself. James Lee, for instance, insisted that, after studying with Bruce, he felt morally uplifted, more honest, and that his whole life was changed. Another of Bruce's pupils was, at the start, shy, timid, quiet, and even bashful. He had learned to fight with all the aggressiveness of a wild animal—and he was able to apply the lessons to ordinary life, coming right out of his shell and blossoming as an individual.''

But how, exactly, did Bruce achieve such results? Danny explains, ''Bruce always tailored his instruction to the personality of the person he was talking to. What he would tell one student— or even an assistant instructor—was always different from what he told another. He thus established a very immediate and intimate link with you. He related everything to a personal basis, taking into consideration a person's height, speed, and so on. Some people kicked fast, others slow, some were better with their hands. So he taught each man to find out his own strengths and to use them. He taught everyone to recognize his own weaknesses, too. He explained also that it was no use any of us try to copy him. None of us possessed the combination of his speed, his rhythm, his flexibility, his timing or even his build. He insisted, 'Man, because he is a creative individual, is far more important than any style or system.' What he set out to do was to liberate people—to liberate them from their own inhibitions. He was both a psychologist and a philosopher—and his students reaped the benefits. I soon realized that I had been preventing myself from achieving my best by being all tensed up and tightened up. The first thing I needed to do was free myself from mental tension.''

Dan makes the point that Bruce ''really set new standards. He was like a Roger Bannister—like an Einstein, Edison or Da Vinci, if you like, so far as the martial arts were concerned.''

Partly as a joke, but mainly in order to get his message across more graphically, Bruce erected a miniature tombstone near the front door of the kwoon. This was adorned with flowers and inscribed on the tombstone were the words ''In memory of the once fluid man, crammed and distorted by the classical mess.'' Bruce once told BLACK BELT magazine, ''That expresses my feelings perfectly.''

BLACK BELT carried a long two-part series on Bruce around this time. At the kwoon in Chinatown, the interviewer, Maxwell Pollard, had a long talk with Bruce and also watched him work out with Dan Lee, one of Bruce's best friends and a brilliant kung

Bruce in the Oakland years. It was during this period that Bruce began to concentrate more on the development of his body. Later the definition of his muscles would become even more outstanding.

Bruce and I at the wedding of student Ted Wong and wife, Krina.

fu man. "Private lessons are usually not interesting," Bruce explained. "It's more enjoyable to teach those who have gone through conventional training. They understand and appreciate what I have to offer. When I find an interesting and potential prospect, I don't charge him a cent," which was true.

The reporter found Bruce moving about the kwoon "like a panther, counterattacking, moving in, punching with great power—occasionally, shin kicks, finger jabs, powerful body punches to the solar plexus, use of elbows and knees." What particularly impressed him was that Bruce's body was constantly relaxed. He thought Bruce's movements those "of a polished, highly refined prizefighter, delivering his blows with subtle economy." His movements seemed to be a "mixture of the wing chun style and Western fencing."

By this time, Bruce's martial arts style had so evolved that he had to give it a name of its own—jeet kune do. He explained that *jeet* meant "to stop or intercept," *kune* meant "fist," and *do* meant "the way or the ultimate reality." It was, Bruce explained, "the direct expression of one's feelings with the minimum of movements and energy. There is no mystery. My movements are simple, direct and non-classical."

There were no sets or classical forms in JKD because they tended to be rhythmic—and so when Bruce sparred, he used "broken rhythm," adding, "Classical forms are futile attempts to 'arrest' and 'fix' the ever-changing movements in combat and to dissect and analyze them like a corpse. But when you're in actual combat, you're not fighting a corpse. Your opponent is a living, moving object who is not in a fixed position, but fluid and alive. Deal with him realistically, not as though you're fighting a robot."

From his own observations he had long ago realized that most forms of kung fu, karate, tae kwon do and other martial arts were based on styles which were basically incomplete. Each had its own forms, movements and so on and each practitioner went into battle believing that he had all the answers, and for that reason Bruce refused to call jeet kune do a "style" which he felt would be to limit it. As a result, JKD possessed neither rules, forms, a set number of movements or techniques with which to oppose other techniques. Its very essence was self-expression, which, in turn, demanded a great deal of self-knowledge. It was not, therefore, a way of fighting that could be easily taught. Many of these realizations sprang from his reading and subsequent understanding of the forces of nature, while others were the product of his own experiences.

At one point, Pollard pressed Bruce to explain what he meant by "directness." Almost before the words were out of his mouth, Bruce's wallet went flying through the air. Instinctively, Pollard reached up and caught it. Bruce said, "That's directness. You did

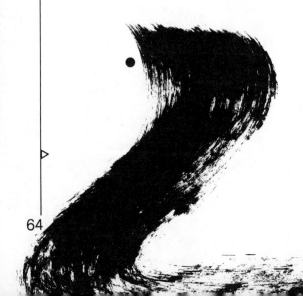

what comes naturally. You didn't waste time. You just reached up and caught the wallet—and you didn't squat, grunt or go into a horse stance or embark on some such classical move before reaching out for the wallet. You wouldn't have caught it if you had. In other words, if somebody grabs you, punch him! Don't indulge in any unnecessary, sophisticated moves! You'll get clobbered if you do and in a streetfight, you'll have your shirt ripped off you." Bruce then gave what he always thought of as a classic definition of jeet kune do. "In building a statue, a sculptor doesn't keep adding clay to his subject. Actually, he keeps chiseling away at the inessentials until the truth is revealed without obstructions. Jeet kune do doesn't mean adding more. It means to minimize. In other words to back away from the inessentials. It is not a 'daily increase' but a 'daily decrease.' Art is really the expression of the self. The more complicated and restricted the method, the less the opportunity for the expression of one's original sense of freedom. Though they play an important role in the early stage, the techniques should not be too mechanical, complex or restrictive. If we blindly cling to them, we will eventually become bound by their limitations. Remember, you are expressing the techniques and not *doing* the techniques. If somebody attacks you, your response is not Technique No. 1, Stance No. 2, Section 3, Paragraph 5. Instead, you simply move in like sound and echo, without any deliberation."

It was about this time that Bruce began to consider abandoning his plans to open a chain of kung fu schools throughout America. A year later, when he had become famous on American TV, efforts were made by important financial interests to persuade him to change his mind and lend his name and prestige to a chain, but Bruce resolutely refused to bargain away his integrity, reiterating that he would run schools only where he could personally supervise the instruction or have it carried on by such assistant instructors as James Lee or Danny Inosanto or Taky Kimura whom he had trained himself—and this, obviously, precluded any possibility of mass instruction for it would take many years to find the right caliber of instructors and to train them properly.

Ed Parker, who has established himself as a leading sifu in the United States, has expressed a fairly firm view about Bruce's success as a teacher. He insists that Bruce himself was "one in two billion," and that God had given him "all the natural talents." But, says Parker, his problem as a teacher was that he could pass on his ideas, but not his talent, so that his philosophy failed to work for the majority of his students. Referring to Bruce's analogy about the sculptor chipping away at the stone, Ed commented, "But if a guy doesn't have the natural talent Bruce had, he can chip all day and he isn't going to find what he had." The problem of being a successful teacher is hardly one that Bruce alone found difficult. Any teacher of any subject finds this true. The very es-

Bruce and kenpo master Ed Parker. Ed would later introduce Bruce to the world of television and motion pictures.

Tombstone which Bruce erected in his Los Angeles kwoon to bolster his views of traditional martial arts training.

65

Bruce practicing with Taky Kimura, the three-sectional staff against the long staff, above, and a blocking and simultaneous striking technique, below. The best defensive move is an offensive one, Bruce would say.

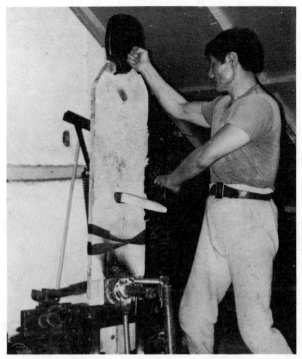
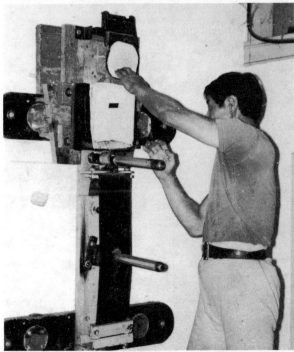

James Lee, a welder by trade, constructing a new piece of equipment and trying it out.

Bruce with members of the Jun Fan Gung Fu branch in Los Angeles.

Bruce practicing a high kick with Dan Inosanto.

	克 強 健 力 學 院 HAK KEUNG GYMNASIUM				
	運動程序 Exercise List.		繳費日期		
	學生姓名 Name BRUCE LEE Sex M Date MAY 27 1965.				

	運動名稱 EXERCISE	組數 SETS	磅 LBS	次數 TIMES	運動名稱 EXERCISE	
1	SQUAT	3	95	10	SQUAT	
2	FRENCH PRESS 1	4	64	6	FRENCH PRESS	TRICEPS
	INCLINE CURL	4	35	6	FRENCH PRESS	
3	FRENCH PRESS 2	4	64	6	PUSH UP	
	"CON" CURL	4	35	6	TRICEP STRETCH	
4	PUSH UP	3	70-80	10	INCLINE CURL	BICEPS
	TWO HAND CURL	3	70-80	8	"CON" CURL	
5	TRICEP STRETCH	3	3	8(6)	TWO HAND CURL	
6	DUMBELL CIRCLE	4	16	INF.	REVERSE CURL	FOREARMS
	REVERSE CURL	4	X64	6	DUMBELL CIRCLE	
7	WRIST CURL 1	4	64	INF	WRIST CURL	
	WRIST CURL 2	4	10	INF	WRIST CURL	
	SIT UP	5	B.W.	12	SIT UP	
	CALF RAISE	5	B.W.	20	CALF RAISE	

此表請勿携出院外 Please do not take it away

When Bruce and I visited Hong Kong in 1965, he had this regimen of weight training.

sence of Bruce's teaching, in fact, was that what might work for him would not necessarily work for the student. However, if he could instill the right frame of mind into the student, then the rest was up to him. He often confessed to me just how difficult this was, commenting, "It is easy to teach one to be skillful, but it is difficult to teach him *his own attitude*."

The great turning point in Bruce's life arrived when he gave an exhibition of kung fu at a karate tournament in Long Beach, California, in 1964. Ed Parker invited Bruce to give a demonstration at the first International Karate Championships. At this time the general public knew very little about the mysterious and secret art of Chinese kung fu, but Ed had known Bruce for some time and was impressed by his abilities. Like many people not well acquainted with Bruce, Ed's first impression had been that he was cocky, but he decided, after seeing Bruce in action, that he "had every right to be—he could make the air pop when he hit."

Bruce's demonstration was viewed by a large crowd which included many leading West Coast karate black belts and instructors. Most people in attendance agreed that Bruce not only had something different to offer, but possessed a unique personality in his own right. As one observer commented, "He had something the others didn't have—you could see it in the way he explained his art, in the way he talked. He was utterly dynamic that night and one couldn't help being drawn to him. Even those who knew very little about the arts found themselves listening to him intently. Luckily, Ed Parker filmed Bruce's demonstration, which was to prove a fortunate break.

In the audience that evening was a Hollywood hair stylist named Jay Sebring—later among the victims of the Manson gang when they invaded film director Roman Polanski's home and murdered his wife, Sharon Tate, and other guests. Sebring, who became a good friend of Bruce's and was instrumental in introducing him to Steve McQueen, was highly impressed with Bruce's vitality and presence. Some time later, while he was cutting the hair of TV producer William Dozier, he mentioned Bruce. Dozier had said he was looking for someone to play the role of Charlie Chan's Number-One Son in a new TV series he had on the boards. Jay mentioned that he had seen Bruce in action and believed Dozier should seriously consider him. He thought he had definite charisma, a great sense of humor, and ought to come across to audiences very well. Dozier took Jay's advice and got in touch with Ed Parker, who took his film of Bruce's demonstration over to the 20th Century Fox studios. Dozier liked what he saw and immediately put in a call to our home in Oakland.

Bruce was out when the call came through and I spoke to Dozier. Although I had never heard of him and he didn't tell me what he wanted, it sounded very hopeful. When Bruce returned his call, Dozier explained that he was interested in him for a new

TV series. Understandably, we were both very excited. Bruce flew down to Los Angeles for a screen test. The reactions were very positive, and Bruce returned to Oakland with high hopes.

With a possible career in Hollywood looming on the horizon, we contemplated what our next move should be. We awaited word from Dozier about his plans for the series. Within a couple of months, the producer had a new project in mind for Bruce. Greenway Productions was already in the process of taping the *Batman* series which would air in the upcoming season. Dozier decided to scratch *Number-One Son* and wait and see what the public's reaction to *Batman* would be. If it was good, then he would follow it up with another series in the same comic book format, *The Green Hornet*. He intended to have Bruce play the part of Kato. All of this meant that Dozier was putting Bruce on hold for a year. In order to secure his services, Bruce was put under options. The option money amounted to $1,800, not exactly a windfall, but it certainly would help out.

Bruce's father had recently died in February of that year, one week after the birth of his first grandson, Brandon. Although Bruce had made a quick trip at the time to attend the funeral, we decided to use some of the option money to make a more leisurely trip to Hong Kong so that his mother and family could meet me and Brandon. Bruce called his mother and told her she could soon expect to see her grandson, "the only blonde-haired, gray-eyed Chinaman in the world," as Bruce kiddingly referred to him. Brandon was born with jet-black hair, but it soon fell out and at three months old he was a real towhead.

We flew to Hong Kong where we would stay in the family home on Nathan Road for four months. It was a difficult time for the family, with Bruce's father having just recently passed away. There were still quite a few people living in the house, and since it was summer, it was extremely hot and humid. Everyone made me feel like a welcome member of the family. I did not receive any of the prejudicial reaction that Bruce had endured with my family. Their attitude was that Bruce knew what he was doing and they would not be able to influence him one way or the other. And they were very proud of their first grandchild. It was, however, a trying time. I could only speak a few words of Cantonese and when Bruce wasn't around, I struggled to understand what was being said and tried to reply, often embarrassing myself and creating moments of laughter. In retrospect it was probably the best training in a language I ever had, similar to learning how to swim by being thrown in the deep end. It was a hard time for Brandon as well because the summer heat and air conditioning frequently caused him to be sick. And since we lived in such close quarters, Brandon couldn't be allowed to cry, or even utter a peep, without being rescued by a well-meaning grandma or auntie. In order not to disturb anyone during the night, I usually

1965
學生體格進度表
BODY IMPROVEMENT LIST

肌肉部份 Parts of Muscles		五月廿七日 Date	七月十日 Date	月 日 Date
頸 Neck		15¼	15½	
胸 Chest	平常 Nor.	39	41½	
	橫張 Exp.	43	44¼	
上膊 Biceps	左 L.	13	13¾	
	右 R.	13½	14¼	
前膊 Fore Arm	左 L.	11	11¾	
	右 R.	11¾	12¼	
腕 Wrist	左 L.	6¼	6¾	
	右 R.	6½	6⅞	
腰 Waist		30	29½	
大腿 Thigh	左 L.	21	22½	
	右 R.	21¼	22½	
小腿 Leg	左 L.	12¼	12⅞	
	右 R.	12½	13	
體重 Weight		140	140	
體高 Height		5'8"	5'8"	

Name: BRUCE LEE Age 24 Sex M

Bruce kept track of his progress. Weight training was a major part of his workouts.

Mrs. Eva Tso.

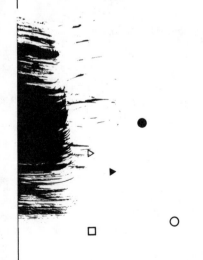

ended up walking the floors with babe in arms into the wee small hours. Consequently, Bruce and I never enjoyed a full night's rest until Brandon was 18 months old.

Bruce wanted so much to show his family what his new wife could do, so he bragged about how I could cook the greatest spaghetti on the face of the earth. When we were first married I hadn't known how to cook a single thing, and then when James Lee's wife died suddenly, I became chief cook and bottle washer for a built-in family, and as a consequence, Betty Crocker and I became best friends. In the few months that had elapsed, spaghetti was about my best creation. Bruce's family was excited about trying it. I was on the spot! My first problem was finding the proper ingredients, not an easy trick in a city that didn't have a supermarket as we know them in the United States. The secret ingredient to my spaghetti sauce was Lawry's packaged mix, unheard of in Hong Kong. A feeling of dread came over me. I managed to get some semblance of ingredients together. While I fumbled in the kitchen, a huge crowd was gathering in the apartment, as relatives from far and near assembled for this special event. The most I had ever cooked for was five, and now there were at least 25 people preparing for this alleged feast. My next problem was that I had never used a gas stove and I didn't know how to regulate the heat. I also didn't realize, until too late, that tomatoes burn easily. Alas, I produced the spaghetti, permeated with the taste of burned tomatoes. To say the least, it was an unmitigated disaster. Poor Bruce! I'm sure his entire family felt sorry for him having married this embarrassingly incompetent person.

We did have some good times during those four months and I became well acquainted with Bruce's family and friends. In particular I should mention a lovely lady, Mrs. Eva Tso, who was like an adopted mother to Bruce. She took Bruce and me everywhere, shopping and seeing the sights. Bruce had a real bond with her and frequently sought her advice about his life and future.

Bruce was keeping in constant touch with William Dozier, awaiting word of the reception of the *Batman* series. The good news was that everything was going great and they fully expected to have *The Green Hornet* in production. The bad news was they had no idea as to "when."

We returned to Seattle in September of 1965 where we stayed with my family for another four months. It was during this stay that my mother really got to know and love Bruce. Then we returned to James Lee's in Oakland. The word from Dozier was always good—"Soon, real soon." Bruce's attitude was that if this thing works out, then fine, but if not, then that would be OK too —he still had his martial arts.

Some of the struggles Bruce had breaking into the film industry read like a scene out of any really grim fight against prejudice. Although he had made 20 films in Hong Kong as a child star, Bruce had never given serious thought to the idea of breaking into American films. He was convinced that the only parts likely to be available to a Chinese were of the "ah-so!" chop-chop, pigtail-coolie-type and he was determined not to lend his talents to that kind of thing. "Everyone admired him for that. He insisted on being human," so said Academy Award-winning screenwriter Stirling Silliphant, one of Bruce's best friends and one of the many well-known Hollywood personalities who became his student, a list which also included Steve McQueen, Roman Polanski, James Garner, producer Sy (Tarzan) Weintraub, Kareem Abdul-Jabbar, and Elke Sommer and her husband Joe Hyams.

When the word finally came through from Dozier that *The Green Hornet* was a "go," Bruce and I moved to Los Angeles in March, 1966, where we found a tiny apartment on Wilshire Boulevard in Westwood. Twentieth Century Fox arranged for Bruce to take a few acting lessons from a coach named Jeff Cory, which was the only formal training Bruce ever had. The accepted opinion of those professionally associated with Bruce throughout his acting career was that he was a "natural."

Based on one of the most successful American radio serials of the 1930s, *The Green Hornet* was intended to show the exploits of Britt Reid, a crusading newspaper editor-publisher who donned green clothes and mask at night and turned crime fighter. As Kato, his manservant and assistant, Bruce was able to give American fans their first glimpse of kung fu. Later Bruce cracked to a newspaper interviewer: "The only reason I ever got that job was because I was the only Chinaman in all California who could pronounce Britt Reid."

Bruce teaching students in the backyard of our Los Angeles home on Roscomare Road.

73

6

"He was not by trade a teacher of screenwriting or psychology, nor was he an ordained minister, and yet he was the greatest teacher I have ever known."
—Stirling Silliphant

"The one important point about Bruce—the thing that needs to be emphasized as much as anything else—was that he himself was constantly learning. I don't think a day went by when he wasn't gathering in some new thing."
—James Coburn

The Green Hornet was not destined to find a place on the list of best television series of all time, although Bruce's role as Kato would, from a historical standpoint, become the most memorable highlight of the show. Today, more than two decades after its debut, I understand that bootlegged copies of the show continue to sell to collectors of Bruce Lee memorabilia for large sums.

Bruce made many personal appearances around the country in preparation for the airing of the series. He made a stunning impression with one Minneapolis critic going so far as to write, "I can tell the producers of *The Green Hornet* how to improve their show, even before it's on the air. What they should do is let the Hornet's sidekick, Kato, write his own dialogue. He's bright and he's funny."

In fact, the show lasted only six months during the 1966-67 season, although there were numerous reruns. Bruce later explained that he thought the series had been played too "straight" to capture an adult audience and that "a lighter James Bond touch," with more time and fewer characters, would have helped.

Although adults found the series corny and farfetched, children everywhere loved Bruce. Even the most scathing critics admitted that Bruce's kung fu was sensational. One critic wrote, "Those who watched him would bet on Lee to render Cassius Clay senseless if they were to put in a room and told that anything goes."

Everyone was impressed by the sheer speed of Bruce's movements. "He strikes with such speed that he makes a rattler look like a study in slow motion," wrote another reviewer. In fact, Bruce had to explain to interviewers that he was forced to slow down his movements so that the camera could catch his actions.

"At first, it was ridiculous," he explained. "All you could see were people falling down in front of me. Even when I slowed down, all the camera showed was a blur."

He told one interviewer, "One of the main characteristics of the show will be the speed of the fights and the simplicity in finishing off the Hornet's enemies." Bruce, I must emphasize, knew as much about showmanship as P.T. Barnum. But there was a limit to how far he would exploit his art. Up to then, most Chinese martial arts films tended to stage long, drawn-out battles to achieve the maximum effect of gore and violence. Bruce, instead, insisted that on any level, audiences would be far more impressed with the sudden, deadly strike, the overwhelming, annihilating effect of kung fu. Provided the essence of his own expression was retained, he consented to a degree of poetic license, which was why viewers saw him perform flying spin kicks and other such dramatic techniques which he would not have considered part of his scientific streetfighting repertoire.

As another interviewer wrote, "The object of kung fu is to send a foe to the nearest hospital in the shortest possible time, what Lee calls 'a maximum of anguish with a minimum of movement.' This is accomplished with knees, elbows, fingers in the eyes, kicks to the head." The same interviewer managed to catch part of the essence of Bruce's multi-sided character and personality when he added, "When he isn't playing the cold-eyed Kato, Lee is the complete ham, alternately the pixie and the tough kid on the block. He puns unmercifully, performs dazzling feats of speed and coordination, wades bravely into the riptides of a language he is trying to master. Sample Lee wit: 'Seven hundred million Chinese cannot be Wong,' or 'I don't drink or smoke. But I do chew gum, because Fu Man Chu.' "

Bruce, like other colorful, bigger-than-life personalities, was delighted by the fame and adulation that came from his appearance in *The Green Hornet*. He basked in the sunshine of personal appearances, and he even rode on processional floats dressed in the black suit, chauffeur's cap and black mask of his Kato role. He enjoyed it all, and yet, was aware that such publicity was only superficially rewarding. His real reward was in providing quality performances. All other benefits, even financial gain, were only icing on the cake.

Bruce in his Kato uniform, signing an autograph for a young man.

Bruce could not help being excited by life and by his own strength and dynamic power, and he wanted people to share in his excitement. Peter Chin, who was an extra on *The Green Hornet* and a life-long friend of the family, recalls that some of the people on the set were put off by Bruce's behavior off screen. "He was always showing people his muscles—showing them how strong he was. I couldn't understand why they got so uptight just because he was strong, just because he wanted to show them what he had been able to do to his body. Not that they ever

Bruce made many public appearances as Kato.

Bruce demonstrating the famous one-inch punch at the Long Beach Internationals.

Working out with Kareem Abdul-Jabbar, Bruce found it a unique and educating experience to practice with his friend whose extremities had such long reach.

A difficult type of push-up, arms extended, using only thumbs.

Part of Bruce's vast library.

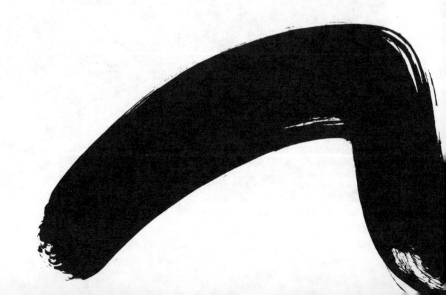

Bruce having a talk with John Saxon, co-star of Enter the Dragon.

Demonstrating a kick on the set of Marlowe *with James Garner.*

said anything straight out to him, but when he had walked away, you'd hear someone say, 'Oh, he's bullshitting—he's a big loud-mouth.' But he wasn't, and that's where they missed the point. He *was* strong. He *was* exceptional.''

In my judgment, Bruce was able to keep a fairly detached view of himself. He knew how good he was. He realized how much he was capable of accomplishing, yet he was not a braggart. ''I'll never say I'm number one,'' he used to tell me, ''but I'll never admit to being number two.''

Above all, he had the saving grace of always being able to laugh at himself. When he was going through a particularly bad period and feeling low, he erected a little sign on his desk which simply said, **WALK ON**. For a time he hung a morbid poster on the wall showing two vultures in the middle of an otherwise blank desert —blank, that is, save for the skeleton of an old cow—and one vulture is saying to the other, ''Patience, my ass! I'm going to kill something!''

Through *The Green Hornet* Bruce first learned what it was like to be a public idol. People fought to get his autograph or even just to touch him. ''It can be a terrifying experience sometimes,'' he told BLACK BELT magazine. ''After a personal appearance at Madison Square Garden at a karate tournament, I started to make an exit, escorted by three karate men. I was practically mobbed as I approached the main lobby, and I had to make a hasty exit through a side door. In Fresno, California, I was scratched, kicked and gouged by riotous fans. I just couldn't protect myself without doing bodily harm to my fans, whose aim, after all, was not to hurt me.''

Yet, for all the success and excitement, the adulation and the autograph signing, Bruce continued to nurture the more studi-ous, more scholarly side of his character. He and Dan Inosanto often spent hours together, browsing through old bookstores. Very quickly, Bruce amassed a colossal library, impelled by an in-satiable desire to learn everything he could about the combative arts. In addition to purchasing books on martial arts styles and as-sorted weaponry, Bruce also had an impressive library on West-ern boxing and wrestling. He wanted a distillation of all that was best and he adapted it to his way of martial arts, jeet kune do. He carried a book with him wherever he went—even when he knew he would get little chance to read it. He had developed the ability to shut out distractions. I frequently saw Bruce sitting quietly reading while there was household uproar all around him—chil-dren crying, doors slamming, conversation taking place every-where. Bruce was even able to read a book while performing a series of strenuous exercises. When necessary, he could insulate himself against everything around him.

Before and after *The Green Hornet,* Bruce spent much of his time giving demonstrations of kung fu. These were at fairs, public parks, club meetings and, most often, at karate tournaments. He showed how to jab with the fingers, and delivered kicks and punches so fast that if anybody in the audience even blinked they probably missed the action. Sometimes he would place his wrists against an opponent's and challenge the man to try to prevent him from hitting him on the chest. Nobody was ever fast enough. This is called *chi sao* (sticky hands), and is part of wing chun training. Bruce often demonstrated this technique blindfolded, depending solely on the pressure, or lack of pressure, he felt with his wrists. He sometimes demonstrated his one-finger push-ups, kicked and broke eight, two-inch boards bound together with tape, and even succeeded in performing one of the most difficult feats in all martial arts—snapping five, one-inch boards dangling in front of him.

On the whole, he disliked these kinds of stunts. He considered them phony and felt they had nothing to do with learning how to defend oneself. Because of this, Bruce rarely indulged in these kinds of stunts, but he did do them once or twice, if only to show that he could do them, and only as a part of his total demonstration. It used to annoy him when he watched other martial artists whose demonstrations consisted solely of such displays. Dismissing the act impatiently, he'd ask, "What's *that* got to do with fighting?"

On the set of The Green Hornet *with James Lee and children, Karena and Greglon.*

Bruce's work on *The Green Hornet* created a welcome change in our financial affairs, at least temporarily. When the series went into production in 1966, Bruce was paid $400 a week ($313 take-home pay), and the first check arrived at just the right moment. We didn't have enough to pay the rent and other outstanding bills.

With the cancellation of the series, Bruce's spirits fell into a low period. I suppose, in a sense, going back to teaching at the kwoon which Dan Inosanto had, in the meantime, kept going, must have seemed a step backwards. Bruce realized that it was time for decisions. There was no way he could run the kwoon full-time and still pursue his film career. With the help of good friends such as Stirling Silliphant, Jim Coburn, Steve McQueen, Sy Weintraub and others, Bruce kept in the public eye with guest appearances on TV shows, such as *Ironside, Blondie* and *Here Come the Brides.* At the very least, they all helped, as they say, to pay the rent.

One of the men who came to Bruce's assistance with good advice at this juncture was the assistant producer of *The Green Hornet,* Charles Fitzsimon. Bruce used to go to lunch with him at Twentieth Century Fox studios and it was from Charles that he discovered the way to make kung fu pay him a satisfactory living wage.

Charles suggested that, instead of relying on the $22 a month Bruce charged for lessons at the kwoon, he should teach students privately—at $50 an hour! Even Bruce was a bit shocked, but

Bruce with Joe Lewis, champion of Jhoon Rhee's tournament in Washington, D.C.

Charles pointed out that Hollywood was full of people who could well afford to pay that sort of money (in fact, Bruce's rates rose to a regular $250 an hour—and people like Roman Polanski even flew him to Switzerland for private lessons).

Earlier on, Jay Sebring had put Bruce in touch with Steve Mc-Queen, who became one of his first celebrity pupils. Bruce and Steve hit it off well together. Bruce found Steve a remarkably apt pupil. Steve had lived a tough childhood himself and had no difficulty relating to Bruce's realistic fighting concepts and principles. Bruce used to say that Steve was a fighter while Jim Coburn was a philosopher. Over the ensuing months, private instruction became one of Bruce's most lucrative and enjoyable activities.

Stirling Silliphant still tells how amazed he was at Bruce's reaction when he first approached him about private lessons. Stirling says that it took him months even to get to Bruce, which he found remarkable when he considered that, as a writer-producer, he often hired actors and Bruce was looking for work as an actor. What was even more remarkable was how, even when they finally did meet, Bruce still refused to play the sycophant. Instead of welcoming Stirling with open arms and playing up to him in the hope of favors to come, Bruce told him, "I think you're too old (Stirling was 49). I don't believe there's a chance your reflexes are good enough to do what I want you to do."

Stirling had been a fencing champion at the University of Southern California and still had incredibly good eyesight and reflexes. "Well, I did a few things and he seemed pleased and rather surprised," says Stirling. Ultimately, he worked for two years with Bruce and earned two certificates of accomplishment. He often says that studying with Bruce changed his whole life and that his writing and living habits underwent a remarkable change. As a writer his mind expanded, his point-of-view on the human condition became more profound and he found it much easier to touch an audience's emotions. "What Bruce taught me is still so much with me, almost a kind of growing thing. He was not, by trade, a teacher of screenwriting or psychology, nor was he an ordained minister and yet he was the greatest teacher I have ever known."

There was also a lighter side to Stirling's training. Our home in West Los Angeles was filled with personalized equipment. Stirling said he was appalled by one stretching device which he thought was as tough as a medieval rack. He once wisecracked to Bruce, "No wonder they talk about Chinese torture."

Another piece of equipment that impressed Stirling was an enormous, soft bag that was set up on the patio—a bag four feet wide and five feet high which required at least two men with outstretched arms to encircle it. "It was like kicking into a giant marshmallow," Stirling recalls, "and one heck of a lot bigger than you. And to think that Bruce could send that thing flying with a single kick!''

Stirling remembers that Bruce insisted that the greatest thing of all to kick at was a large palm tree. ''He used to tell me, 'When you can kick so you aren't jarred, but the tree is jarred, then you will begin to understand a kick.' ''

It was during this period that some of the greatest karate men came to Bruce for personal instruction. ''Three of Bruce Lee's pupils, Joe Lewis, Chuck Norris, and Mike Stone, have between them, won every major karate championship in the United States,'' reported *The Washington Star.* ''Joe Lewis was grand national champion in three successive years. Bruce Lee handles and instructs these guys almost as a parent would a young child, which can be somewhat disconcerting to watch.''

Perhaps among the greatest tributes to Bruce's teaching and mastery came from Chuck Norris and Joe Lewis. Chuck went on TV and stated to millions that Bruce was his teacher and that he considered him ''fantastic'' while Joe Lewis, on being awarded the heavyweight crown, publicly thanked Bruce for the improvements he had achieved while under Bruce's training. Louis Delgado told BLACK BELT magazine, ''I have never seen anyone who has baffled me so completely. I am in total awe whenever I spar with Bruce.''

Bruce with our Great Dane, Bobo.

James Coburn vividly describes what it was like to be a student of Bruce's. He had already been taught karate by an experienced teacher for his role in *Our Man Flint.* ''That first day Bruce and I went out back and started going through a few punches and things, hits and side kicks and so on, so he could find out where I was. We started working in earnest the following week and worked three solid days a week for the next five months. I was interested more in the esoteric aspect, while he was immersed in the total—the esoteric and physical. His method of teaching was not teaching at all in the accepted sense—it was evolving through certain ideas, teaching you tools, finding out your strong points, your weak points. Our getting together lasted over five years. I'd have to go away on location at times, but each time I came back I was astonished to observe how Bruce had evolved even further. The steps he had taken in between times were really giant steps.

''He always had this energy,'' Coburn continued. ''It was always exploding on him, though he channeled it whenever possible, which was most of the time. I mean he actually created this energy within himself. He always got more force from doing something, for instance. We'd work out together for an hour and a half and at the end of that time, he'd be filled with force. You really felt high when you finished working out with Bruce. He was always trying to bring everything down to one thing—one easy, simple thing. There are, in fact, no complicated methods in jeet kune do—anyone, really, can do them. But it was the perfection. We'd do a thing Bruce called 'bridging the gap.' It's the dis-

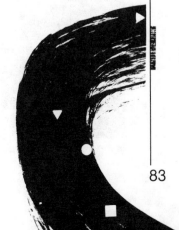

Bruce with actress Sharon Tate on the set of the Dean Martin movie which Bruce choreographed.

tance from your opponent you have to stand in order to score—it's how close you can get in, in other words, and move away fast enough not to get hit in return. It amounts to constant observation of your opponent and constant observation of yourself, so that you and your opponent are one—not divided.

"And while you were picking up this physical bridging of the gap," Coburn went on, "you were learning to overcome certain psychological barriers at the same time. And the one important point about Bruce—the thing that needs to be emphasized as much as anything else—was that he, himself, was constantly learning. I don't think a day went by when he wasn't gathering in some new thing. He'd be bursting with enthusiasm about some new kick he'd just invented—'Bang! Bang! Look at that, man!' he'd shout. And I'd try it and the flow of energy was always, well, like a whip—always relaxed until right at the end, all the force came out—TUNG!

"So far as kicks were concerned, we did a lot of work with big bags. I remember once I got a brand new bag, about a 100-pound thing hung up with a big L-iron. Bruce thought it was a little too hard—'that's not really the right kind for you,' he said, 'but we'll work with it today anyway—maybe I can soften it up a bit for you.' So he took a running side kick at it and broke the chain! I mean that thing hung on a 75-pound chain—and he broke that chain and busted a hole in the canvas—it flew up in the air and fell out in the middle of the lawn out there—in tatters, dilapidated—a brand new bag. Wow! And the things he could make you do! I mean he told me there was no trick to breaking boards, that I could easily do it. So he told me 'Take off your shoe' and I did so —and then he showed me how to use my heel—and bang! sure enough, it would feel sensational—the board went. Then Bruce would say, 'Right, man, now let's get down to some real work, eh?' "

Stirling Silliphant never had any doubts that Bruce was star material. But it was one thing spotting star quality, and quite another finding the right plots and stories for Bruce—and the right people to back him with hard finance. In the great majority of Hollywood movies there are not all that many parts for a Chinese man, so something special had to be created for Bruce, even in light of the fact that, at this stage, he still wasn't what the financiers viewed as a "bankable" property. When Stirling wrote a love story for Columbia called *A Walk in the Spring Rain*, he actually wrote in a fight sequence. But as he explains, "The problem was that the scene was set in the Tennessee Mountains. Well, there weren't any Orientals in the story, because they just didn't have any Asians down there. But I brought Bruce down to Tennessee to choreograph the fight. There were two stuntmen on the picture, who were very skeptical of Bruce. Here they were, big, tough, Caucasian cats, and Bruce weighed in at 135 pounds, a

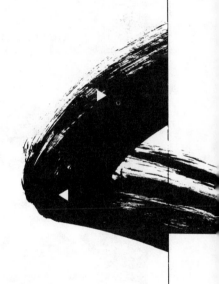

Bruce and Chuck Norris. Chuck played the villain in The Way of the Dragon.

Bruce in about 1966 with a kicking shield constructed by student Herb Jackson. Note the definition of his abdominal muscles has improved from earlier years.

rather gentle and smooth-looking Chinese man who didn't look all that tough. In fact, he always maintained a very cool and low profile. The fellows resented my bringing in an outsider to stage the fight. I made it clear to them that since I was the producer and writer of the picture, Bruce was the boss on their fight.

"The guys kept putting Bruce on, so finally I said, 'Why don't you just give them a little sample of what a side kick can do?' Bruce had his air shield with him and so he said, 'One of you guys hold this shield. I'm going to give it a little kick. But I suggest you brace yourself first, you know, I kick pretty hard.' They went through their 'sure, sure' routine. So I told Bruce to make it really interesting and do it beside the swimming pool. If those guys are so tough and can take it with their backs to the pool, OK. But if he kicks as hard as I think he can, and they aren't really braced, well, it'll knock 'em right into the water.

"Everybody said, 'Cool, man.' So with no movement—no run, nothing, just standing there—he kicked this guy right through the air and out into the middle of the pool. Then the other guy had to prove himself, too. So he braced real low. And *sshhp* . . . again! Bruce lifted him off his feet, up into the air and out into the deep end! Well, those guys scrambled out of the pool Christians! And from that moment on, those guys loved Bruce."

7

Marlowe, starring James Garner, was Bruce's first appearance in a Hollywood full-length motion picture. "Two of the best sequences had Bruce in them," says Stirling Silliphant who wrote the script. "In one, he came in and tore up Garner's office. In the other, he met Garner on the roof of the Occidental Building in Los Angeles and took a header, kicking and screaming off into space."

Aside from the money Bruce received from his work on *Marlowe* and the residuals from *The Green Hornet,* the period between 1967 and 1971 was a difficult time for us financially. As a result, Bruce returned to teaching full-time at the kwoon, as well as privately. It was a stressful period for him because he wanted so desperately to provide well for his family.

Up to 1968 we had always lived in apartments or rented houses. We had already moved four times in the space of our two years in Los Angeles, and now with Shannon on the way we decided to buy a house. How we ever thought we were going to pull this off is amazing to me now, but it was both scary and exciting at the time. Such daring moves are best left to the young and foolish or to those who dream big. And that was Bruce and I in 1968 —young, foolish, and with grand visions.

We were very naive about house shopping. My mother had recently sold our family home in Seattle for $28,000. It was a beautiful brick, five-bedroom house. Bruce and I said to ourself that it would be great to find a house like that in Los Angeles. We didn't know much about the housing market in Southern California. When I first approached a realtor about finding a house in the mid-$20s, I was not prepared for the kind or location of property available for that sum of money. Eventually, Bruce and I realized that we would have to upgrade our housing budget.

"You just wait. I'm going to be the biggest Chinese star in the world."

—Bruce Lee

Bruce delivering a kick to James Garner's head for the film Marlowe.

Bruce preparing to break five dangling boards. He maintained that this kind of "trick" did not prove one was a good fighter, merely a good showman.

When we first looked at the house at 2551 Roscomare, we were somewhat disappointed because it needed a lot of work. Steve McQueen, who was a student of Bruce's at the time, came over to look at the house, and he even had his business manager consult with us about the deal. Everyone agreed it was a steal. The house cost us $47,000. With the mortgage payments, property taxes and insurance, we were in way over our heads. Friends assured us that with the tax refund we would receive, it was still better to own than to rent. It was a struggle to hang onto it, but I must say we sure did have some fun in that house. When I look back at my life with Bruce, it was the years before he became a major star that were the happiest for both of us. Struggling, hoping, wishing, and working for common goals created a strong bond between us. I am sure it is this way with many couples.

Our house was a pretty interesting sight to an unsuspecting visitor. We couldn't afford a couch for the living room but we did have an antique opium bed that once belonged to Bruce's father. It was beautiful with inlaid marble and teakwood and was as big as a queen-size bed. This became our living room sofa. We could get the whole family, plus more, on the bed at the same time.

On the patio, under the eaves of the house, hung various pieces of training equipment. There was a huge red hanging bag, a top and bottom bag, a square hitting pad strung by elastic cords, a squat machine, a leg-stretching device, a variety of weights and assorted kicking and striking pads. Bruce and his students frequently worked out in our large, flat backyard.

Brandon was about five years old at the time, just beginning kindergarten and starting to make a few neighborhood friends. One of his friends, Luke, frequently invited Brandon to play at his house but he would rarely come over to our house. I asked Luke's mother why he was reluctant to come over and she confessed that Luke was afraid of all the strange things at our house and the people yelling and hitting each other. Brandon just accepted all this activity as part of growing up, but I guess the Lee household was rather strange to his friends.

Bruce's training regimen was going along smoothly until a certain day in 1970 when he disregarded a part of his routine with what would turn out to be fateful consequences. On this particular day, for whatever reason, Bruce failed to warm up properly before beginning his weightlifting routine. He began by doing what is called a "Good Morning" exercise. Placing a 125-pound barbell across his shoulders, he bent over at the waist and then straightened up. At the time, he felt just a mild twinge of pain in his lower back. In the next few days the pain became severe, causing him to use heat and massage and then eventually to seek out a doctor. Over the next few weeks he underwent extensive examinations. The final diagnosis was that he had injured his fourth sacral nerve, permanently.

The doctors advised him to rest in bed and no working out. They told him to forget kung fu, that he would never kick again. Instantly, a black cloud of depression settled over him. Bruce stayed in bed flat on his back for three months and after that, another three months of just moving around the house—from desk, to chair, to bed. With all that I've mentioned about his personality, his energy, his dreams, I'm sure one can imagine what a desperate time this was for us. It was like keeping Jonathan Livingston Seagull in a canary cage.

Although he was severely depressed by physical inactivity, Bruce refused to accept the doctor's opinion about the permanency of his injury. Throughout his life, he was an avid believer in the power of positive thinking. He kept believing he would heal, always believing, as if the belief itself would make it happen. In the meantime, if his body could no longer soar with the eagles, then his mind could, and so during the next six months he wrote constantly, putting into words his training methods and his philosophy of JKD. From the vast collection of books he had amassed on all forms of combative arts and philosophy, he read and made notes. Many of these books, which I still have, are heavily underlined and inscribed in the margins with his comments on how a particular key passage could be applied to JKD.

Even though it was a dispiriting period in his life physically, and with financial worries compounding the situation, he used this time to grow as a person and as a martial artist. Bruce was never satisfied to just imbibe knowledge for its own sake, rather he insisted upon transferring his thoughts into action. Eventually, his notes occupied eight, two-inch volumes which he thought he might one day publish. Later he decided against publication based on his belief that readers might construe "his way" of martial arts to be "their way." After his death and after much contemplation on my part, I condensed his notes into a volume called *The Tao of Jeet Kune Do,* published for Ohara. I simply felt there was too much value in his writing to be buried forever.

Six months passed. Bruce found he could no longer endure the sedentary life. He began to test the waters, working out moderately at first, and resuming his teaching duties. Although his back remained a chronic source of pain for the rest of his life, his will was greater. He simply "decided" it would not stand in his way, so he pushed on from there, and began once again to lead what appeared to outsiders to be his normal life-style.

Although from a physical standpoint Bruce began to regain his energy, the psychological pressures on him were intense. Perhaps the worst of these was a sense of frustration. He had all these tremendous ideas and drive and he was very sure he could be an important force in world films. He believed that via the medium of film, he could give the gift of kung fu to the world.

"Bruce, you're great, and you'll be really super when you do a

Cracking five dangling boards on Hong Kong television.

Stirling Silliphant, left, Bruce, and James Coburn, far right, traveled to India to scout locations for The Silent Flute.

film or something like that,'' people would tell him. They probably meant it kindly, but their very faith in him, the knowledge that he was not alone in thinking himself a great talent, intensified his frustrations rather than ameliorated them. The Hollywood movie structure agreed that Bruce possessed great personality and charisma, but felt he simply did not have enough screen credits, and ''he was Chinese''—and it was difficult to persuade the financiers to risk their money on a relatively unknown Asian. This was emotionally very difficult for Bruce to accept. The very notion brought back many bad memories of the racial persecution he had endured from the British when he was a child living in Hong Kong. In sharp contrast, Bruce, himself, never harbored any racial prejudice against anyone. He had been even willing to fight a fellow Chinese man earlier in San Francisco for his right to teach kung fu to white students, or students of any other color for that matter. Regardless, in his heart he never did blame the producers and financiers and used to say to me that movies were not an art, but were, instead, a combination of commercial creativity and creative commerce.

Nevertheless, if the mountain wouldn't come to Muhammad, then Muhammad would go to the mountain. Bruce realized that the only way of breaking through the barriers that prevented him from becoming a success in Hollywood was to accept a secondary or co-starring role in a production associated with the martial arts. Once he was actually on the screen, once the motion picture public had seen the marvels of kung fu as only he, himself, could portray it, then and only then, would he begin to realize a major part of his ambitions. In his mind, the idea for *The Silent Flute* was born.

It was natural that Bruce should seek the help of Stirling Silliphant and James Coburn when he first conceived the idea of the film story based on the martial arts. Both were his pupils and had, for a long time, acted as his unofficial advisers with regard to film and TV roles. Moreover, all three had wanted to do ''the definitive film'' on the martial arts for a considerable period of time. So in early 1969, they hired a writer to develop a script from Bruce's treatment. The final product, unfortunately, bore no resemblance to Bruce's original concept and contained none of the ingredients they were all after. So it was turned over to another screenwriter. Again it didn't work out. In desperation the three men decided to sit down together and write the script themselves. It was a labor of love, for they had no guarantee of production. For the next few months they met every Monday, Wednesday and Friday from 4:00 to 6:00 p.m., having pledged that they would allow nothing to interfere with that schedule—''without fail or excuses, above work and family, until it was done.'' Stirling then gave the first draft a final polish and sent it to Warner Brothers. The studio liked it, but made the provision that the film

In his 1970 trip to Hong Kong with Brandon, Bruce talked to a television audience.

be shot in India where they had a large sum of "blocked rupees" (money their films had earned in India which the Indian government refused to remit to the U.S.). Although India was nobody's idea of the right locale for a Chinese story, the three men intrepidly set off, hoping for the best. Jim Coburn was to be the "name" in the film but Bruce, who was to play five different roles, would unquestionably dominate the story. Altogether they spent three weeks in India, trying to find the right place.

India, of course, is an old home of the martial arts and Bruce was very eager to see the caliber of artists living there. One day Bruce went out to meet a bunch of Indian practitioners and he started off by saying, "Now, let's see where you're at—what you can do."

"Then, all of a sudden," as Jim Coburn said, "it was utter chaos. There were nine guys and they just started beating the hell out of each other. Within minutes one guy was streaming blood from his mouth. Bruce held up his hand and shouted, 'No, no! Hold it a minute! Look, this is what I mean.' So without any warm-up, Bruce gave them a little demonstration. They were absolutely awestruck. They had no conception of this kind of thing. When he finished, they all went down on their knees. I mean that."

The idea, of course, was that if satisfactory locales could be found, some of the Indian martial artists would be used in the film, and thus reduce the below-the-line budget considerably. "No way," Bruce told his partners. "It would take me at least three years to train any of those fellows to the right level."

Three weeks in the intense heat, with constant traveling and increasing feelings of frustration, coupled with the realization that the trip was bound to prove abortive, helped to create a friction among the three men. Stirling recalls that it was the first time he realized that Bruce was just as capable of an ego trip as any other actor. The trouble was that at all the big hotels James Coburn got the "star" treatment from the management whereas both Bruce and Stirling had to be content with lesser accommodations. One evening Bruce could no longer contain himself and complained to Stirling that they deserved at least equal treatment. Stirling says it didn't lessen his respect for Bruce, but merely made him see Bruce in a more realistic light. Hitherto, Bruce had been the sifu and philosopher. Now, here he was declaring impassionately that one day he would be a bigger star than either James Coburn or Steve McQueen. "I told him there was no way he could be that," says Stirling. "That he was a Chinese in a world run by white men. But I was wrong—and how! For in the end, he went out and proved himself."

The Silent Flute contained many of the themes that reflected Bruce's life and behavior. The script traced a young student's evolution through the martial arts—his problems of ego, his new-

Having a discussion with his partner and co-producer of Enter the Dragon, *Raymond Chow.*

Bruce shows James Franciscus how to perfect his kick on the set of Longstreet.

found courage in facing the abyss of death, and finally his spiritual rebirth. At one point in the script, Bruce says "I'm not even sure what trials I passed through or how I came to be here. I still have doubts, many doubts. How, without more struggle, can I resolve them?"

Bruce was very excited at the prospect of doing *The Silent Flute* because he thought it was an ideal role for his debut as a major star. He had predicted that kung fu would win worldwide popularity and he believed he was the right man to introduce it to the world through the medium of film. He desperately wanted that film to be made, but, eventually, Warner Brothers decided that it could not be done in India and jettisoned the project.

A few years later, by which time Bruce had become an international sensation with offers pouring in from all over the world, Jim and Stirling tried to revive it. They flew to Hong Kong to talk over the project with Bruce. This time, however, it was Bruce who had to say no. I think Stirling and Jim were somewhat affronted by Bruce's decision and even felt that he was snubbing them. After all, it was Bruce who had started the whole project. But, by that time, there were too many other demands on Bruce. Everybody wanted him and the role itself would have been a backward step for him. There was never any question of resentment so far as Bruce was concerned. But the situation had changed and he believed that Jim and Stirling, being two experienced professionals themselves, would have been the first to recognize that their own decision would have been similar had they been placed in Bruce's circumstances. Certainly Jim and Stirling never lost their admiration and affection for Bruce. Jim was not only among the pallbearers in Seattle, but delivered the eulogy.

Years after Bruce's death, *The Silent Flute* was made into a film or, I should say, a film was made that had some semblance to the original script. It was called *Circle of Iron*, and starred David Carradine in the role that Bruce would have played. Screen credit was given to Bruce in the form of "Story Originated by Bruce Lee." Perhaps the producers thought that adding Bruce's name to the credits would embellish the movie's appeal. I'm sure Bruce would have wished they had not bothered, since the final product was far removed from anything he had envisioned.

By 1970 the state of the family economy was relatively grim. We had pinned high hopes on *The Silent Flute*, and it had seemed that the realization of that project was always just around the corner. But when it failed to materialize, and with Bruce's back injury, our prospects of solvency were quite dismal. That's when I decided I had to go to work. Bruce was adamant in his opposition to the idea. My main job was to be wife and mother and to Bruce it was a disgrace for his wife to work. In the end, however, we could see no other way out. I got a job at an answering service, noting on the application as past experience my secretarial chores in my husband's business, which was true enough. I worked evenings from 4:00-11:00 while Bruce watched the kids. We never told anyone that I was working, and had an elaborate scheme of reasons for why I was not at home if anyone called or came over. When I came home at night, Bruce was usually asleep because his back was quite painful, but he would often leave me beautiful notes of love and appreciation, which made it all worthwhile.

Shortly after returning from India, Stirling and Bruce got together to work on a TV series called *Longstreet*. "We worked out the opening story together," says Stirling. "It was called 'The Way of the Intercepting Fist' (that's a literal translation of jeet kune do). James Franciscus starred as a blind detective. Bruce played an antique dealer who saves Jim from being clobbered by some toughs trying to force him off the dock. Of course, the blind man wanted to know how he did what he did. Bruce's character refuses because the motivations of revenge are wrong. So, the story dealt with getting the blind detective's head together by teaching him the way of the intercepting fist. For instance, when James Franciscus asks Bruce to teach him kung fu, Bruce replied 'I cannot teach you. I can only help you explore yourself.' Later on, he tells Longstreet, 'You must learn defeat—like most people you want to learn to win.'

"We had more fan mail on that episode than any other in the series," recalled Stirling. "I like to think that that episode was his first good film—the first to show him off to the world as an Oriental martial artist with pride and dignity. On that first *Longstreet*, Bruce was shown as a perfect teacher, the mystic simplicity of his lessons really came through. It is still one of the best martial arts shows I've ever seen on the air. I say that even though I wrote the final script."

Prior to the filming and subsequent airing of *Longstreet*, Bruce, along with five-year-old Brandon, took a quick trip home to Hong Kong to see Bruce's mother and arrange for her to live in the United States. When Bruce arrived there, his first trip back since our visit in 1965, he was completely stunned by his reception. He had absolutely no idea of how famous he had become in Hong Kong. He simply had not realized that *The Green Hornet* had been one of the most popular TV shows in Hong Kong and throughout Southeast Asia and, as a result, he had become a great popular hero. Now he returned to find every Chinese breast swollen with pride at the achievement of the hometown boy in America. Newspapers demanded interviews, radiomen stuck microphones in front of his face and he was invited to appear on Hong Kong's two TV channels. The old films he had made as a child star were now among the most popular offerings on these channels. As Jim Coburn puts it, "He was like the King of Hong

Kong. And when he appeared on TV he just about killed everybody.''

Bruce put on a stunning performance for Hong Kong television. All his charm, charisma and wit came to the surface that night. Then he got up and gave a supercharged demonstration of his art. Five, one-inch boards were dangled in the air and Bruce leaped up and sidekicked them and broke four! While the audience was still howling with applause, Bruce led Brandon out and he broke some boards, too.

The great reception he received in the city where he was reared undoubtedly played a part in Bruce's eventual decision to return to Hong Kong. "After I left Hong Kong," Bruce revealed to FIGHTING STARS magazine, "the media there kept in contact with me by telephone. Those guys used to call me early in the morning and kept the conversation going on the air so the public was listening to me. Then one day, the announcer asked me if I would do a movie there. When I replied that I would do it if the price was right, I began to get calls from producers in Hong Kong and Taiwan. The offers varied from U.S. $2,000 to $10,000.''

The first episode of *Longstreet,* Bruce's "Way of the Intercepting Fist," hit American TV screens with sizzling impact. It was so good that producers of the show decided to open their fall schedule with it—that highly competitive time of the year when networks vie for top ratings with their new season's offerings. Bruce, by virtue of Stirling's subtle script, had an opportunity not only to demonstrate the lethal effectiveness of kung fu but was able to get across some of the philosophical principles which lay at the foundation of his art.

The reviews in the trades and the big newspapers, such as the *New York Times* and the *Los Angeles Times*, were almost without exception excellent. They were very different from anything Bruce had ever earned as Kato, whose kung fu techniques had been highly acclaimed, while Bruce the actor had been largely ignored. This time, the accent was on Bruce's acting ability, which pleased him immensely. "It was the first time in my life I had any kind of review for my acting," he told FIGHTING STARS.

Perhaps that show, more than any other, convinced Bruce that his dreams had real validity, that he was not merely deluding himself. He reiterated his fierce conviction of his own ultimate success to anybody who would listen. He had an endearing habit of making prophecies—and so that no one could ever accuse him of being wise after the event, he always committed them to paper. I still have one written about this time (early 1969) which is uncanny. Entitled "My Definite Chief Aim," it reads:

> I, Bruce Lee, will be the highest paid Oriental superstar in the United States. In return I will give the most exciting performances and render the best of quality in the capacity of an actor. Starting in 1970, I will achieve world fame and from then onward till the end of 1980 I

will have in my possession $10,000,000. Then I will live the way I please and achieve inner harmony and happiness.''

Bruce's fan mail after the *Longstreet* episode was considerably more than other members of the cast. Hollywood studios and producers really began to sit up and take notice. Even before this, Warner Brothers had started to catch on to the fact that the art of kung fu had captured the public's imagination and decided to launch a TV series based on the martial arts. Bruce himself had been working on the idea of a Shaolin priest, a master of kung fu, who would roam America and find himself involved in various exploits. The studio contacted him and he was soon deeply involved. He gave them numerous ideas, many of which were eventually incorporated in the resulting TV success *Kung Fu,* starring David Carradine.

Jim Coburn and Bruce on their Indian sojourn.

The *Kung Fu* series became a source of mixed feelings for Bruce. He had long talks with Jim Coburn who advised him, ''Man, you go into TV and you're going to burn out your show in a season. Television chews up genius—it can chew a man up in a series of 13 episodes—it's a waste of time. Set your sights on Hong Kong, instead.''

Bruce would come home and relate to me what Jim had said. Still, the idea of a nationwide television series was unquestionably attractive and Bruce, at the time, would have liked to have done it. In the end, of course, he was glad he had not. It did surprise us, however, that Warner Brothers never offered it to him. I guess we thought that since Bruce had contributed so much to the original idea, and since he had ignited the enthusiasm of a number of people working on the project, that he might be included in the realization of the final product. Later we were informed that neither Warner Brothers nor ABC-TV had even considered starring him in the series. They thought he was too small, too Chinese, that he wasn't a big enough name to sustain a weekly series, and that he was too inexperienced.

A short time later Bruce learned through a friend in Hong Kong that a film offer was on its way from Run Run Shaw, a movie mogul from Shanghai who had escaped to Hong Kong in the late 1940s. The Shaw Brothers almost singlehandedly founded the highly successful Hong Kong film industry and built a chain of theaters throughout Southeast Asia. When the offer finally arrived, Bruce laughed. Run Run's offer was U.S. $2,000 a film and Bruce knew Shaw would expect to sign him to a long-term contract. At one stage, however, Bruce did go so far as to wire Shaw asking about script details and other matters. Shaw's reply was a paternalistic, ''Just tell him to come back here and everything will be all right.'' This sort of attitude definitely rubbed Bruce the wrong way. He simply could not conceive of himself as being ''owned'' by Run Run Shaw.

Regardless, and despite his irritations with the Hollywood

Bruce greeting Mr. and Mrs. Stirling Silliphant in Hong Kong. Raymond Chow is on the far right.

Bruce practicing flying kicks over the Indian desert.

movie structure, Bruce still thought his future lay in America. Then, out of the blue, came a second offer. Raymond Chow, formerly a producer of long-standing for Run Run Shaw, had in 1970 decided to launch out on his own and had formed Golden Harvest Productions. It was a move which led to bitter rivalry between Shaw and Chow, further aggravated when Chow made a determined approach to Bruce.

Throughout his time in Hong Kong, Bruce repeatedly made it clear that he was not interested in local film politics. He was not taking sides in the fight between Run Run Shaw and Golden Harvest or any other independent producers. He was primarily concerned with his own interests. With considerable business acumen, Raymond Chow dispatched one of his senior producers to further discuss the matter with Bruce in Los Angeles. This was Mrs. Lo Wei, wife of one of his top directors. In and of itself the money was not all that attractive, $7,500 per film. Not all that great by Hollywood standards, but good by Hong Kong standards. There was to be no long-term contract—the contract was for two films only. While considering the contract, Bruce spent a great deal of time reviewing the most recent Mandarin movies. As he said later, "They were awful. For one thing, everybody fights all the time, and what really bothered me was that they all fought exactly the same way. Wow, nobody's really like that. When you get into a fight, everybody reacts differently, and it is possible to act and fight at the same time. Most Chinese films have been very superficial and one-dimensional."

There was some further "politicking" necessary before Bruce was prepared to sign the contract with Raymond Chow. Run Run Shaw was still vying for Bruce's services, so Raymond decided that rather than allow Bruce to set foot in Hong Kong, where he might be snatched from under his nose, the star should fly direct to Bangkok where the film was to be shot. Bruce refused. He was determined to make it clear that he was not about to be anyone's pawn. So in July, 1971, Bruce landed in Hong Kong. He stayed at the airport only long enough to greet a friend and make some phone calls, then flew on to Bangkok.

Shortly after he had signed the contract with Raymond, a Taiwanese producer telephoned him in Thailand. "The guy told me to rip up the contract, and he'd top Raymond's offer and even take care of any lawsuit for breaking the agreement," Bruce later told a magazine. Such men had little concept of Bruce's character and intelligence. Once he had signed his name, that was that. Besides which, he had almost a sixth sense, as his lawyer Adrian Marshall confirms, about offers, the kind of men who made them, and the degree of say and authority he might be able to exert.

And so on a hot and humid day in July, Bruce found himself in the little village of Pak Chong north of Bangkok. It was here that he met Raymond Chow for the first time. The two men shook hands and afterwards were able to laugh at Bruce's first words. With sublime assurance and the utmost confidence, he declared, "You just wait, I'm going to be the biggest Chinese star in the world."

Raymond and Felicia Chow helped celebrate my 26th birthday at dinner in Hong Kong.

8

"The future looks extremely bright indeed, with lots of possibilities ahead—big possibilities. Like the song says, 'We've only just begun.'"
　　　　　　　　　　　　　—Bruce Lee

Bruce's first letter to me from Pak Chong revealed the whole picture. "Bangkok was fine. However, Pak Chong is something else. The mosquitoes are terrible and cockroaches are all over the place. The main reason for not having written is for lack of services, but also, I had a rather nasty accident—as I was washing a super thin glass, my grip broke the damn thing and cut my right hand rather deeply—the worst cut I've had—it required ten stitches. Don't worry, though, I am sure within two or three weeks I will be OK, though it is inconvenient for me to write (or take a bath or anything) for the past week.

"I have got to find out the confirmation of you people coming—though I am pretty damn sure. They want me to do a short film on JKD in exchange for your fare. I'm in no condition to do it but I'm sure they won't want to press matters because since my arrival, everyone including the Shaw Brothers, is calling and using all means to get to me. One thing is for sure, I'm the superstar in Hong Kong . . . I'm writing rather poorly due to my hand —it's much better now. I'm taking my vitamin pills and though I'm down to 128 pounds I'm getting used to the conditions here —the cockroaches are a constant threat, the lizards I can ignore—I just want you to know I miss all of you and am sending my love to all . . . take care my love. Love and kisses . . ."

There were all sorts of troubles: "Another director (a fame lover) just arrived, supposedly to take over the present director's job. It really doesn't matter, as long as he is capable as well as cooperative . . . The food is terrible, this village has no beef and very little chicken and pork. Am I glad I came with my vitamins. I wish you were here because I miss you and the children a lot. This village is terrible. No place like home. I'm looking forward to meeting you in Hong Kong. . . . My personal love to my wife . . . and Brandon, Shannon.''

On July 28, he wrote: "It's been 15 days since my arrival in Pak Chong and it seems already like a year! Due to lack of meat, I have to get canned meat for lunch. I'm glad to have brought along my vitamins. I miss you a lot but Pak Chong is no place for you and the children. It's an absolute underdeveloped village and a big nothing.

"The film I'm doing is quite amateur-like. A new director has replaced the uncertain old one; this new director is another so-so one with an almost unbearable air of superiority. At any rate, I'm looking forward to leaving Pak Chong for Bangkok where it is at least halfway decent. Then I'll fly to Hong Kong and make the necessary arrangements for you people to come over—looking forward to seeing the three of you very much indeed.

"My voice is gone (very hoarse!) from yelling and talking under really terrible conditions—machines running, ice cutting, etc., etc. Anyway, all hell broke loose here. My back is getting along fair—needs lots of rest after a fight scene. Have to go and eat now—see if I can find any meat. Love to you my dearest wife. With kisses.''

Another letter:

"Haven't heard from Paramount—maybe September is a little bit too late for returning for *Longstreet*—time will tell. Can you send some pictures of you and the children?

"The future looks extremely bright indeed, with lots of possibilities ahead—big possibilities. Like the song says, 'We've only just begun.'

"I have a feeling Stirling won't be able to finish the script in time for me to come back in September. At any rate one way or another, I really don't mind too much, the Lee family is enjoying some nice moments ahead. My love to you my dearest.''

Another:

"Linda, to make sure of arriving in the States on time, I've gone through two days of hell. I sprained my ankle rather badly from a high jump on a slipped mattress—which required a drive of two hours to Bangkok to see a doctor—consequently I caught the flu (Bangkok is hot and stuffy and the traffic is a 24-hour jam). Anyway, with fever, cold aches and pain, we used close-ups while I dragged my leg to finish the last fight.

"I feel all right now except for my ankle and am doing well in Bangkok . . . I can tell you one thing, things are happening too damned fast here.

"Well, at least at the Thai Hotel I have breakfast in bed, nothing like Pak Chong. By the way I picked up a his and hers 'something' for both of us. It's a surprise for our anniversary. You will have to wait for me to bring them to you.

"Happy anniversary, my sweet wife!''

Enclosed was a short note for Brandon, printed out in capital

Shannon sits in my lap while our dog, "TeRIFFic" licks my ear. Riff was the brother of Steve McQueen's schnauzer.

Bruce used to say that Shannon walked like a lady from the day she could get up on her two feet.

Bruce and Brandon in Hong Kong—1970.

The Lee family in front of our Los Angeles home—1969.

letters:

"Hello Brandon! When I come back we will go to the toy shop. Love you my son, Dad.

P.S. Will you kiss Ma Ma and Shannon for me?"

Again:

"Linda, I'm writing this letter to let you know that: A) *Longstreet* is such a success that reaction is instantaneous whenever my character comes up. B) So Paramount is asking me to reappear and stay as a recurring character. C) So that means I might get a one-month leave after September 1st and fly back to finish the second picture. D) Of course, that means killing two birds with one stone and getting extra bread. E) I've already wired Tannenbaum for him to let me know of his 'arrangements' for me."

More:

"My dearest wife, today, I've sent the telegram. However, it won't be till Monday Tannenbaum will receive it, unless there is extra service in the studio during the weekend.

"Anyway, what it amounts to is a few more days of wondering how it will turn out. Disregard the consequences. I am firm on my ground of 'it's about time to raise my worth.' Well, it's a matter of whether I'm coming back to meet you and then fly together to Hong Kong or you and the kids flying over to meet me in Hong Kong. I have to say the first choice is more profitable and full of possibility. Time will tell.

"Though I have to say the house payment troubles me somewhat. I'm sure you will find the best possible way out. I hate to have an overall change of payment.

"Anyway, my future in acting has now begun. I'm sure the one I'm doing now will be a big success—again, time will tell. Though the place I'm in is rather hell, I'm in the profession where I belong and love to do.

"Take care my love. It won't be long for us to be together."

Another:

"Linda, by now, you should have received my letter regarding hoping to extend the loan or the best way, whatever is might be.

"Received telegram from Paramount extracted as follows:

Freelance offer for not less than three episodes at one thousand per episode. Each episode, not to take more than three days from Sept. 5 to Sept. 30th—1st class round-trip ticket—imperative we hear from you immediately to prepare script for the character you portray.

"Well, here is my answer:

My usual two thousand per episode plus quality technical advising. If acceptable can start work from Sept. 7 to Oct. 7. Notify immediately for schedule arrangement.

"Really, if Paramount really likes me and if I really did such a good job, I feel I should advance to at least two grand per episode,

Bruce playing with Brandon and Shannon in his study.

Brandon shows Shannon what to do on their first day of school in Hong Kong, 1971.

Determined-looking Brandon with his dad, 1970.

Brandon screams down the slide in a Hong Kong park.

disregard three days or anything. Let's face it, my billing isn't exactly there. Who knows what the future holds? I feel rather definite about this, don't you?

"There comes a time when you have to advance or retreat—this time I can always retreat to my Hong Kong deal."

These had been extraordinary weeks for both of us. I found myself involved in all the excitement as the desperate Paramount executives, unable to trace Bruce by telephone or cable, sought me as an intermediary. Once that first episode of *Longstreet* had appeared, all the world, it seemed, suddenly wanted to talk to Bruce. First it was Run Run Shaw, then independent producers and finally Paramount. "They couldn't get me because I really was in the sticks," Bruce explained to reporters later. "It's funny, but when Paramount sent telegrams and telephoned Hong Kong for me, boy, the producers there thought I was an important star. My prestige must have increased threefold."

I quit work when Bruce went to Hong Kong to make the first movie. Our financial burdens and my working were the primary motivating factors that convinced Bruce to sign with Golden Harvest. He was paid $15,000 to make two movies, enough to bail us out of our troubles, but not enough to allow us to keep the house by refinancing a large balloon payment. We sold it in 1972 for $57,000—it was still a "fixer-upper."

A short while later, Bruce finalized the deal with Paramount and returned to Hollywood to appear in three more episodes of *Longstreet*. The difficulty was that these three episodes had been written before "The Way of the Intercepting Fist" aired. Faced with Bruce's success, Stirling was asked to somehow work him into the succeeding episodes. As fate would dictate, Stirling could do little more than create walk-through parts for him. That first episode had been one of the finest showcases Bruce could have hoped for. His role in the next three episodes, therefore, seemed to him anticlimatic.

The Hollywood movie structure had seen the light. Both Paramount and Warner Brothers (the same studio that had nixed *The Silent Flute* and then had raised his hopes about the *Kung Fu* TV series only to abruptly dash them) rushed in with option offers. In October, 1971, Warner Brothers made the following proposal:

1. 25,000 (U.S. dollars) for which WB to receive an exclusive hold on his TV services in order to develop a project for him.
2. If we go to pilot, the following fees would be applicable against the 25,000 dollars:
   a. Half-hour pilot—10,000
   b. One hour pilot—12,500
   c. Ninety-minute pilot—15,000
   d. Two hour pilot—17,500

If for any reason we did not make a pilot, it might be a good idea to apply the 25,000 toward a feature deal.

3. Series Prices
   a. Half-hour—3,000 per original telecast—scale residuals.
   b. One-hour—4,000 per original telecast—scale residuals.

The offers were both flattering and inviting. It was at this time that Bruce, certain that he stood at the threshold of success, again consulted Jim Coburn, who repeated his advice about TV "chewing up geniuses" and that Bruce should pin his hopes on Hong Kong instead. The problem was that although *The Big Boss* (released throughout most of the world as *Fists of Fury*) was ready for distribution, it had yet to be premiered. And although Bruce knew he had done well, he had never seen the film's final edit and therefore had no guarantee of what the public reaction would be.

Bruce had not really reached any firm decisions when he returned to Hong Kong after completing the *Longstreet* episodes. His contract with Raymond Chow called for a second film, *Fist of Fury*. His intentions were, vaguely, to finish this film for Chow, then return to Hollywood and consider several of his television offers. The children and I accompanied Bruce back to Hong Kong. I'll never forget our arrival at the Hong Kong airport. Bruce had told me that there would probably be some people meeting us at the airport, so as we approached our landing in Hong Kong I changed my clothes and prepared to meet whomever was there to greet us. Nothing could have prepared me, however, for the masses of fans and reporters that applauded Bruce's return. A group of Boy Scouts held up a banner to greet us, flashbulbs were going off everywhere, and the crowds of people threatened to become a security problem for the airport police. It was my first exposure to what it was going to be like to be the wife of a movie star, and it filled me with pride as well as some trepidation about how our lives were changing and this was before *The Big Boss* had even premiered.

Shortly after our arrival in October of 1971 we experienced a wonderful night when we attended the midnight premiere of *The Big Boss* in Hong Kong. Bruce was nervous about the premiere because Hong Kong audiences are notorious for expressing their approval or displeasure about new movies very vocally. But that night every dream that Bruce had ever had came true as the audience rose to its feet with thunderous, cheering applause. In less than two hours of action on the screen, Bruce became a glittering star, and as we left the theater we were absolutely mobbed. One American entertainment critic wrote, "That film is the finest action job of Bruce Lee's career. It is one of the most outstanding examples of sheer animal presence on the celluloid ever produced. I would match it against the best of Clint Eastwood, Steve McQueen or the various James Bonds."

Within three weeks, the take at the box office was ahead of the previous record-breaker, *The Sound of Music*, which had grossed $2.3 million in Hong Kong in less than nine weeks. In fact, *Boss*

Brandon and Bruce pose in front of comical caricatures.

Some of Bruce's extended family, aunts, uncles, and cousins in Hong Kong. Bruce's elder brother Peter is to his left.

This was the house with the big garden where we lived in Hong Kong.

Attending the premiere of Fist of Fury, *Raymond Chow, left, director Lo Wei, fifth from left.*

Attending the gala charity premiere of The Way of the Dragon.

Brandon demonstrates his board-breaking prowess.

In these two photos, Bruce, Brandon, and I appear on a telethon to raise funds for victims of a typhoon disaster.

Bruce at Golden Harvest Studios in Hong Kong.

Hong Kong audiences delighted in watching Bruce break boards. It wasn't a part of a serious martial arts demonstration, but Bruce would perform these tricks to amuse viewers.

took in over $3.5 million in Hong Kong alone within 19 days, after which it proceeded to smash all records throughout the Mandarin circuit and in cities as far away as Rome, Beirut and Buenos Aires. "We knew from the outset that the film was going to be a success," Bruce told reporters, "but I have to admit we weren't really expecting it to be that successful." He explained that he hoped the film would represent a new trend in Mandarin cinema. "I mean people like films that are more than just one long, armed hassle. With any luck, I hope to make multilevel films here—the kind of movies where you can just watch the surface story if you like, or can look deeper into it. Most of the Chinese films to date have been very superficial and one dimensional. I tried to change that in *The Big Boss*. The character I played was a very simple, straightforward guy. Like, if you told this guy something, he'd believe you. Then, when he finally figures out he's been had, he goes animal. This isn't a bad character, but I don't want to play him all the time. I'd prefer somebody with a little more depth."

Golden Harvest installed Bruce and I and the children in an apartment, or flat as it is called in Hong Kong, in the Waterloo Hill area of Kowloon. It was a small place with two bedrooms, a living and dining room, and a Chinese kitchen. A lot of the modern conveniences that I had been used to, such as a washer and dryer, were missing. Our clothes were washed by hand and hung out the window on bamboo poles to dry. The windows had bars on them for security reasons as do most houses in Hong Kong, even though our flat was on the 13th floor. The building was equipped with elevators, but they frequently broke down and we would all have to trudge up and down the 13 floors. Actually it got to be sort of fun, so Bruce and I used to run up and down the stairs for exercise. Our neighbors thought we were a bit strange.

Soon after our arrival a man named Wu Ngan came to live with us. He had grown up with Bruce in the Nathan Road household as the son of the servant who lived with the Lee family. He lived with us during our entire stay in Hong Kong, and when he was married the following year, his wife also lived with us and later his children. The Wu family spoke no English nor did any of their numerous relatives. This forced me to learn Cantonese very quickly and after a short while I could get along fairly well in the language. At this time, Brandon was six years old and Shannon was two. Brandon was soon enrolled at La Salle College, the same school Bruce had attended years earlier. Even though the administration had not been too pleased with Bruce's academic prowess back in those days, they were willing to give Brandon a chance. The classes were taught in English but all the boys were Chinese so Brandon quickly picked up Cantonese while playing on the grounds. Shannon attended nursery school as it was very important to get her started early in order that she might pass the entrance tests into kindergarten later. By the age of three, she was wearing a uniform, carrying a book bag, and learning Chinese characters. Both Bruce and I felt that it was important for the children to learn the Chinese language and customs as well as American, and what better place to do it than in Hong Kong.

Bruce quickly became immersed in the filming of *Fist of Fury* (renamed *The Chinese Connection* for U.S. distribution). Most of it was shot at the Golden Harvest Studios and largely at night. It was not uncommon for Bruce to come home at three or four in the morning. One of Bruce's ideas for *Fist* was to bring a friend and student, Bob Baker, over from California to play the part of the Russian heavy. His character was well received by the Chinese audiences, thus laying the groundwork for the use of other Caucasian bad guys in future films.

Once again there was an enormously successful premiere for *Fist of Fury*. A few days later, Bruce and Bob discreetly snuck into the balcony of a theater to watch the film unnoticed. Bruce wanted to judge the audience's reaction and perhaps pick up comments which might later prove useful. As the movie played, the audience made very little noise, but at the end they were in a frenzy and began clapping and clamoring. "The fans in Hong Kong are emotional," Bob commented after the screening, "If they don't like the movie, they'll cuss and walk out. When the movie came to an end, there were tears in my eyes. All I remember is shaking Bruce's hand and saying 'Boy, am I happy for you!' "

And so with the release of *Fist of Fury*, Bruce's career soared to even greater heights, smashing box office records everywhere. Within 13 days, it had topped *Big Boss'* record of H.K. $3.5 million and zoomed toward the $4-million mark. Not all the critics took a kindly view of the film, however. Even the *South China Morning Post* (a British newspaper) criticized the handling of the film by director Lo Wei but claimed that when Bruce "lashed out, he does it beautifully. The fierce fighting in fits of blind anger is frightening—and superb." In fact, Bruce himself had become noticeably disenchanted with Lo Wei during the making of the film and their "feud" was well publicized. Bruce's only concern was to make a quality film and he was genuinely annoyed that there wasn't a proper script and that production techniques were almost chaotic. He thought Lo Wei didn't seem to be interested in what was going on and at one stage was actually discovered listening to a horse race on the radio when the actors were supposed to be playing out a romantic love scene.

And yet, the success of the film was really never in doubt because on a least two levels it delighted Chinese audiences. Aside from the fact that Bruce was considerably more dramatic in this picture than in *The Big Boss*, his fighting was more lethal than ever. In addition to his dynamic unarmed fighting techniques, he

Bruce and director Lo Wei.

Bruce and Lo Wei surrounded by Thai children during the filming of The Big Boss.

The Big Boss *was filmed in the small Thai village of Pak Chong.*

Having fun on the set of The Big Boss.

employed the nunchaku for the first time with sensational effect, using the sticks "with horrifying accuracy and bravado," as one critic reported. Bruce's use of nunchaku, however, also led to some unfavorable criticism. Their use is banned in many parts of the world, and in some states in the U.S., even their possesion is a felony. "I had to use some sort of weapons," Bruce pointed out. "After all, that guy is coming at me with a sword, and no man can use bare fists against a sword. At any rate, the use of the sticks is based in history since guns were not used in those days." Aside from this realistic point of view, Bruce was creatively intrigued by the dramatic and theatrical appeal of the nunchaku. His library contained many books about weapons, both ancient and modern, Oriental and Western, and he saw the nunchaku as historically justified, and no more likely to encourage youngsters to violence than the use of a rifle by John Wayne in a Western.

In *Fist of Fury* critics applauded Bruce even further for knowing how to raise a laugh by making fools of his enemies. "He's an actor with a sense of the absurd," noted the same critic admiringly. Yet paradoxically, it was that very plot that made Bruce a hero to millions of Chinese. It appealed to their desire for self-respect in a way that is inexplicable to people living in Western countries who have never been exploited.

The film opens with the death of the teacher of a Chinese martial arts school in Shanghai around 1908. At the funeral, representatives from a Japanese martial arts school present a tablet to "The Sick Man of Asia." Bruce not only resents the insult but, believing the Japanese were responsible for the teacher's death, decides to avenge his honor. In the end, Bruce challenges the top Japanese expert and knocks the stuffing out of both him and the giant Russian. When at one stage, Bruce roars defiantly "Chinese are not sick men!" audiences erupted from their seats. Literally. Historically, they were reminded of the Japanese invasion of China and the subjugation they experienced. By necessity the Chinese have had to be a violent people. Bruce himself was concerned with this aspect. "The glorification of violence is wrong. That is why I insisted that the character I played in this film should die at the end. He had killed many people and had to pay for it." Chinese audiences hated his death and many protested, outraged that their hero should be punished.

Phil Ochs, a member of the legendary New York folk music circle of the early 60s, has described how he "sat entranced" for five hours when he first viewed Bruce's films in the Philippines. "I could hardly believe my eyes. I had seen the Japanese samurai movies, but was not prepared for what was to come. The stories were simplistic and based mainly on revenge. They always involved fighting schools and a revered master teacher. 'I will teach you to be the best fighters in the world, but you must never use it to harm anyone unless absolutely necessary.' Near the beginning is the act of outrage; the insults of a rival school, the poisoning of a master, the murder of a loved one. Lee, the hero, the best fighter, demands vengeance and is always restrained until he can hold himself in no longer. Then follows the most exciting action ever filmed for the screen. One man against 50 with no weapons. He begins to wade his way through the lesser villains with his fists, his elbows, his feet. There are no camera tricks. The members of the audience are hysterical, clapping, cheering, sometimes leaping to their feet. When he gets to the major villains it becomes a dance of extraordinary beauty (one reviewer said that Bruce made Rudolf Nureyev look like a truck driver). It is not the vulgarity of James Arness pistol-whipping a stubbled, drunken stage robber; it is not the ingenious devices of James Bond coming to the rescue, nor the ham-fisted John Wayne slugging it out in the saloon over crumbling tables and paper-thin imitation glass. It is the science of the body taken to its highest form. And the violence, no matter how outrageous, is always stangely purifying. The face and mind of Bruce Lee are as important as the action. The expressions on his face as he psyches out his opponents are beyond description; at times he is lost in ecstasy, almost sexual, and when he strikes, the force of the blow is continued by his mind and the look of concentration and satisfaction is devastating.''

As a result of this sort of reaction to his films on an international scale, Bruce suddenly found himself in urgent demand by film makers everywhere, which soon led him to declare in a publicity release, ''These films should do for me what the spaghetti Westerns did for Clint Eastwood.'' An influx of martial artists suddenly poured into Hong Kong, hoping to duplicate Bruce's ''luck.'' He was not impressed. ''They think they can be lucky, too. Well, I don't believe in pure luck. You have to create your own luck. You have to be aware of the opportunities around you and take advantage of them. Some guys may not believe it, but I have spent thousands of hours perfecting what I do.''

Bruce is greeted at the Hong Kong airport upon his return from the States in 1971. Next to him is his co-star in The Big Boss, Maria Yi.

Bruce relaxes in the Hong Kong countryside, early 1970s.

117

9

Bruce's second film made him the hottest show business property in the Far East. In the Philippines the film ran for over six months and the government there finally had to limit the amount of foreign imports in order to protect their own domestic producers. In Singapore, as in Hong Kong, scalpers made a fortune out of the film, charging 18 times the price of a ticket. On opening night, thousands of fans rushed the theater, causing such an immense traffic snarl that the showing had to be suspended for a week while the police worked out new traffic arrangements.

Moreover, producers throughout Southeast Asia began offering Bruce money, some making their offers through the medium of newspaper headlines. "I had a heck of a problem," admitted Bruce to FIGHTING STARS. "I had people stop by my door and just pass me a check for $200,000. When I asked them what it was for they replied, 'Don't worry, it's just a gift to you.' I mean, I didn't even know these people. When people pass out big money—just like that—you don't know what to think. I destroyed all the checks but it was difficult to do because I didn't know what they were for. Sure, money is important in providing for my family, but it isn't everything." He became totally suspicious of everyone. It was a very disconcerting time. "I didn't know who to trust and I even grew suspicious of my old pals. I was in a period when I didn't know who was trying to take advantage of me."

Once Bruce had finished *The Big Boss* and *Fist of Fury,* he was on his own and under contract to no one. The success of *Boss* and *Fist* made Bruce aware that he must make a picture that would merit a greater public response and at the same time command more respect in the martial arts world. He had seriously considered another Golden Harvest script, *The Yellow Faced Tiger,* yet insisted that there should be a professional script along Hollywood lines if he were to do the film. Bruce had always been dissatisfied with the way films were made in Hong Kong where the directors more or less make up the stories as they go along, often based (but never acknowledged) on the plot lines of fantasy stories which are popular in Asia, similar to the stories in Western comic books. When Lo Wei refused to agree to a professional script, Bruce bowed out. It was a risk but, as Bruce often commented, "greatness requires the taking of risks, that's why so few ever achieve it." Instead, he decided to form his own production company, Concord, and work in partnership with Raymond Chow.

From the very beginning, Bruce felt that in Hong Kong, producers considered moviemaking to be merely packaging up goods, like groceries, and shoving them across the counter to the customers. "Everything is overplayed in Mandarin films. To make really good ones, you'd have to use subtlety, and very few people in the business want to risk any money by trying that. On top of which, the scripts are pretty terrible. You wouldn't believe all that stuff I rewrote for *The Big Boss.* All of us have to come secondary to the quality of the film itself." To further illustrate the point, the following excerpt is reproduced from an article written by Bruce in his early adult career:

On the set of Enter the Dragon *with Jim Kelly.*

> This article expresses my personal true beliefs, a sort of personal view of the motion picture industry and the ideas of an actor as well as a human being. Above all, I have to take the responsibility to myself and do whatever is right, my time must be devoted to preparation of the role . . . after that comes money. To the business people in films—and I have to say that cinema is a marriage of art and business—the actor is not a human being but a product, a commodity. However, as a human being, I have the right to be the best god damn product that ever walked, and work so hard that the business people have to listen to you. You have that personal obligation to yourself to make yourself the best product available according to your own terms. Not the biggest or the most successful, but the best quality—with that achieved comes everything else.

> An actor is, first of all, like you and me, a human being who is equipped with the capablity to express himself psychologically and physically with the realism and appropriateness, hopefully in good taste, which simply means the revelation of the sum total of all that he is—his soul-searching experiences, his idiosyncrasies, etc. Just as no two human beings are alike, the same holds true for an actor.

> An actor is a dedicated being who works damn hard so that his level of understanding makes him a qualified artist in self-expression—physically, psychologically and spiritually. I regard acting as an art much like my practice in martial art because it is an expression of the self.

> As an actor I am frustrated between business and art with the hope that through harmonious reconciliation of these I can then come out expressing myself and truthfully communicating.

Bruce and Raymond Chow in Rome for the filming of The Way of the Dragon.

Dedication, absolute dedication, is what keeps one ahead—a sort of indomitable obsessive dedication and the realization that there is no end or limit to this because life is simply an ever-growing process, an ever-renewing process.

An actor, a good actor that is, is an artist with depth and subtlety. Indeed, what the audience sees on the screen is the sum total of what that particular human being's level of understanding is. If he is ready, well-prepared, radiating tremendous force of energy, and honest confidence of expression, working hard to grow and expand oneself in one's own process, well, this person is professional, an "efficient deliverer" in my book.

Clearly Bruce's view of acting, that it was merely a vehicle for self-expression, closely paralleled his approach to his martial art. And as with his martial art, quality was paramount to all else.

"Ever since I was a kid, the word quality has meant a great deal to me," Bruce once told a reporter. "The greatest satisfaction is to hear another unbiased human being whose heart has been touched and honestly says, 'Hey, here is someone real!' I'd like that! In my life, what can you ask for but to be real, to fulfill one's mission, and above all, actualize one's potential instead of dissipating one's image, which is not real and expending one's vital energy. We have great work ahead of us and it needs devotion and much, much energy. To grow, to discover, we need involvement, which is something I experience every day, sometimes good, sometimes frustrating. No matter what, you let your inner light guide you out of darkness."

Bruce further made clear his beliefs in an interview with the *Hong Kong Standard*. He explained, "I'm dissatisfied with the expression of the cinematic art here in Hong Kong. It's time somebody did something about the films here. There are simply not enough soulful characters here who are committed, dedicated, and are at the same time professionals. I believe I have a role. The audience needs to be educated and the one to educate them has to be somebody who is responsible. We are dealing with the masses and we have to educate them step by step. We can't do it overnight. That's what I'm doing right now. Whether I succeed or not remains to be seen. But I just don't feel committed, I am committed."

He argued that with regard to violence, "I didn't create this monster—all this gore in the Mandarin films. It was there before I came. At least I don't spread violence. I don't call the fighting in my films violence. I call it action. An action film borders somewhere between reality and fantasy. If it were completely realistic, you would call me a bloody, violent man. I would simply destroy my opponent by tearing him apart or ripping his guts out. I wouldn't do it so artistically. I have this intensity in me that the audience believes in what I do because I do believe in what I do. But I act in such a way as to border my action somewhere between reality and fantasy."

Bruce posing in period Mandarin costume at the Shaw Brothers Studio.

Bruce interviews several actors for his directorial debut in The Way of the Dragon.

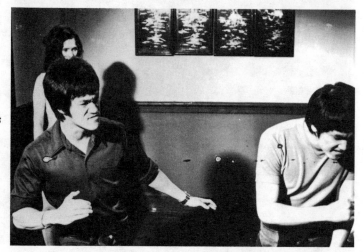

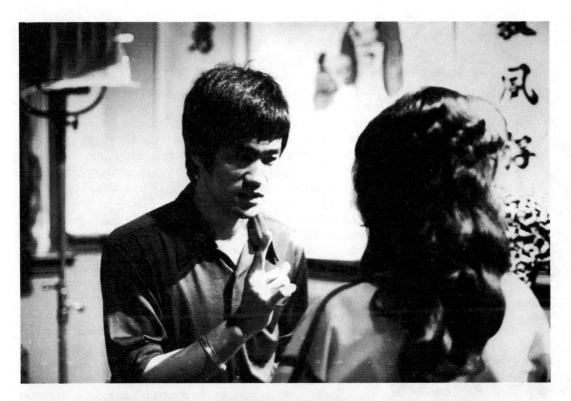

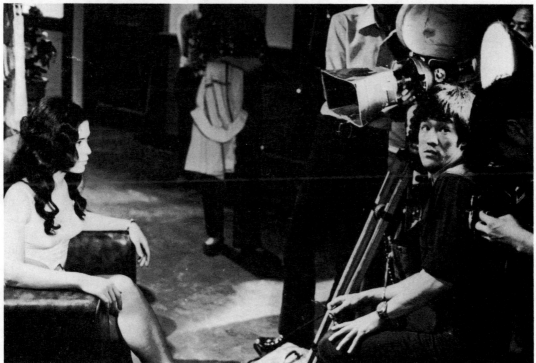

Bruce as director. He wrote, directed, and starred in The Way of the Dragon.

With The Way of the Dragon, *his third Hong Kong film, Bruce began to put his own stamp on his films.*

In that same interview he revealed that, as both an actor and a human being, he would like to evolve by playing different roles, yet thought it would be impossible in Southeast Asia because he had become too typecast. "Besides, I can't even express myself fully on film here, or the audiences wouldn't understand what I am talking about half the time. That's why I can't stay in Southeast Asia all the time. I am improving and making new discoveries every day. If you don't you are already crystallized and that's it," and Bruce made a slashing gesture across his throat. "I'll be doing different types of films in the future, some serious, some philosophical and some pure entertainment. But I will never prostitute myself in any way."

Paramount to all else, Bruce felt it essential that he put his own stamp on his films. During this time he reread his collection of numerous books on filmmaking, ultimately concluding that the only way he could be assured of protecting his own personal and creative integrity would be to write, direct, produce and star—in reality to do the whole thing himself. This was an extraordinarily daring decision, one which would demand from him tremendous creative energy. Historically speaking there have been scores of highly creative and talented individuals who have placed themselves in this so-called hyphenate position and have watched their careers plummet into the abyss as a result. Regardless, once Bruce made his decision he assumed full responsibility and plunged into the work courageously like a man possessed.

Behind his decision was a strong conviction that each successive character he played should possess a uniquely different personality. He realized that people wanted to see him as a fighter, yet insisted emphatically that each of the characters he portrayed be one of great depth. Previous to Bruce, no other actor in Hong Kong had ever taken such a step. He was as great a nonconformist with regard to Mandarin films as he was with the martial arts. He was an innovator, a creator, a man who shaped events rather than one who was shaped by them.

Bruce finally hit on the main idea underlying the script for *The Way of the Dragon* (released as *Return of the Dragon*), and subsequently made numerous trips to scout locations and spent hundreds of hours discussing the project with the assistant director at our house. I sat in on most of these dialogues, but as the conversations were generally conducted in Chinese, it was difficult to follow their rapid speech, even though my Cantonese had improved considerably. Later, when we were alone, Bruce and I would talk over his ideas in English, which often served to spark new ideas in him.

From the beginning, Bruce was aware that moviemaking was a mixture of art and commercialism. Bringing the U.S. karate champions Chuck Norris and Bob Wall to Hong Kong and Italy was an aesthetic decision as well as a commercial one. The truly commercial aspect was that the audience to which he was trying to appeal was Chinese—and the Chinese like to see their Chinese heroes conquering people of a different race. If that sounds like racial prejudice, perhaps it is understandable in view of the history of the Chinese people. But just as important to Bruce was the fact that he would be fighting professional karate men rather than actors or dancers, which he believed would give his film greater realism and authenticity. To many who saw the film it may have seemed strange that a film about Chinese kung fu should be set in Rome, with the climax taking place in that ancient home of the gladiatorial arts, the Colosseum. But when Raymond Chow, Bruce's partner in film, mentioned that he had a contact there who could arrange for equipment, locations and production details, Bruce at once spotted the uniquely aesthetic possibilities inherent in such a marvelous setting.

Bruce in a meditative mood in Hong Kong.

There were problems of logistics, time, permits and innumerable other difficulties to be overcome in Rome. They filmed on the streets, at the airport, around Rome during heavy traffic hours and even during bad weather. In addition, the shooting schedule was a grueling 14-hour day, seven days a week. On one day in particular they shot an almost unbelievable 62 set-ups in the Rome airport alone. Undoubtedly there were some who felt that Bruce was difficult to work with in that he constantly demanded perfection in himself and everyone around him, but he knew what he wanted and how to get it. Admittedly he was very blunt and outspoken when he felt it necessary, but all things considered, he kept himself on a totally professional level throughout the entire production.

Bruce found fight scenarios fascinating. His martial arts choreography was a highly skilled art in and of itself. At home we had a videotape recorder attached to the television so he could tape Western boxing and wrestling matches. He also purchased video footage of championship fights, particularly those of Muhammed Ali. He ran these, and others, through his hand-editing machine, studying combat techniques, constantly thinking ahead to the fight scenes he might use in his films. In the three films he did up to and including *The Way of the Dragon*, for instance, there were about 30 fight scenes, each being unique and fitting the character's personality and situation. After everything was choreographed on paper, the fights were tried out with real opponents. This resulted in further adjustments being made to allow for such parameters as the adversary's strength, height and so forth. The last big duel with Chuck Norris took 20 pages of written direction and was as carefully planned as a professional ballet performance. Bruce worked it all out in our study at home, often with me playing Chuck Norris. He would get a sudden inspiration and yell, ''Come on, let's try this,'' and then we'd try all the movements again, often working together into the morning.

125

Bob Baker, a villain in Fist of Fury, *stands in front of a San Francisco Chinese theater where* Fist *was playing.*

With Bruce's increasing popularity, fans often mobbed him, requiring police protection.

There was another outstanding innovation in *The Way of the Dragon*. Most Chinese films use canned music for their scores. But this one had its own special score with Bruce personally sitting in on one recording session and playing a percussion instrument. He had a supervising hand in everything—the dubbing, set design, costumes, editing—literally everything. By the time the final product was completed, he must have seen the film several hundred times in bits and pieces and in various stages of development, both in his mind as well as on celluloid.

The Way of the Dragon was initially intended for distribution in Southeast Asia only. Bruce's original idea in making the film had been to show another side of himself to Hong Kong audiences. Since he had no intention of aiming at the world market, he constructed and produced a story with which primarily Chinese people could identify. He wrote an appealing main character, that of a naive country boy trying to adjust to situations he encountered in a crowded foreign capital. Through this character he was able to show a very humorous side of himself, a side which had never appeared before in any of his films. Bruce drew a great deal from his own personal experiences in writing this character, recollecting those first days when he had returned to San Francisco, his birthplace, from Hong Kong. There is a lot of the real Bruce Lee in that film.

When the film was finally released, it ran into a new situation in Hong Kong—censorship. A new anti-violence campaign had been launched (and, indeed, was copied by Singapore which heavily censored all violent Mandarin-language films, including *The Way of the Dragon*). Fortunately the censors insisted on cutting only one small scene (which was restored for overseas distribution) where Bruce lands five consecutive kicks to Chuck's head. It was a beautiful movement, an important part of the way the viewer is led into the psychology of the fight, and Bruce was disappointed that it was cut.

Bruce made a wager that this film would outgross his first two films, at least in Hong Kong. He forecast that it would take in more than H.K. $5-million. Nobody could believe it—almost three times as much as *The Sound of Music*! The press, when they heard of his wager, began to tease him unmercifully. Bruce threw himself into the fun of it and was like a kid in his delight when *The Way of the Dragon* finally topped the $5-million mark. Inevitably, it broke every record ever established on the Mandarin circuit.

Amidst all the glory and adulation, there was a price to pay and Bruce was being handed an increasingly larger and larger bill on an almost daily basis. "The biggest disadvantage," Bruce admitted to BLACK BELT "is losing your privacy. It's ironic but we all strive to become successful, but once you're there, it's not all rosy. There's hardly a place in Hong Kong where I can go without

Shannon and I greet Bruce upon his returning from filming Way *in Rome.*

being stared at or people asking me for autographs. That's one reason I spend a lot of time at my house to do my work. Right now, my home and the office are the most peaceful places.''

He explained that he avoided social gatherings wherever possible (he had never liked them, in fact, even before he became famous). "I'm not that kind of cat. I don't drink or smoke and those events are many times senseless. I don't like to wear stuffy clothes and be at places where everyone is trying to impress everybody else. Now, I'm not saying I'm modest. I rather like to be around a few friends and talk informally about such things as boxing and the martial arts. Whenever I go to such places as a restaurant, I try to sneak in without being detected. I'll go directly to the corner table and quickly sit down, facing the wall so my back is to the crowd. I keep my head low while eating. No, I'm not crazy. I only look like it. You see, if I'm recognized I'm dead, because I can't eat with the hand that I have to use to sign autographs. And I'm not one of those guys that can brush people off. Now I understand why stars like Steve McQueen avoid public places. In the beginning I didn't mind the publicity I was getting. But soon, it got to be a headache answering the same questions over and over again, posing for photos and forcing a smile.''

In sharp contrast, there were undoubtedly the nice things. From a material standpoint, we had certainly moved up a rung. We were able to move out of our small flat on Waterloo Hill into a large house in the nearby Kowloon Tong area. Individual houses are rather rare in Hong Kong and we were fortunate to be able to find one. The red Porsche Bruce had purchased in California when we really couldn't afford it, was replaced by a sporty Mercedes 350SL. He had a gold Rolls-Royce Corniche on order by the time he made his fourth and final film. He always had a desire for good-looking, powerful cars which he drove with a passion. Bruce also had a fondness for stylish clothes, and in Hong Kong's numerous boutiques, he could indulge himself. He had some fun with this sort of activity, but in truth he rarely had time to go out shopping because of his work, nor did he have the inclination after a while because of the problem of being recognized. One of his greatest passions was for books although he refused to regard them as material possessions. Instead, he saw them as repositories of ideas, philosophies, and spiritual principles. Whether we were rich or poor, Bruce always went to great lengths to collect books, many of them rare first editions.

Being able to provide a nice home for his family and a few more of the comforts of life certainly took some pressures off Bruce, yet he still did not feel totally secure within himself about his financial future. The reason for this was that the money we were spending was being advanced to us from Concord Productions (Bruce and Raymond's company) on the strength of profits that were not yet realized from *Way of the Dragon*. That made it doubly important that *Way* be successful. And so while some stresses in Bruce's life were decreasing, other tensions were accelerating.

In all honesty, Bruce never placed much importance on material possessions. They were not what he desired from life. Certainly, he wanted security, for that spelled independence, which meant that he could pursue excellence. And it was excellence, quality, achievement, progress, that he really wanted. He thought of money as something that would accrue to him as a matter of course if he achieved quality. He never felt he could ignore it, but making money wasn't his primary aim. He could see money, possessions and all the rest of the apparatus of success in their true perspective.

Neither was Bruce a name dropper, and having lots of famous friends meant absolutely nothing to him. He used to say, "the best carpenter is just as important as the man who's made an important film." Even before he became famous, he felt himself the equal of anyone else around him and he never felt any sense of inferiority because he was Chinese or because he wasn't a millionaire. He never looked at life in quite that way. Much of this may have had something to do with the fact that he was going to be a great success one day. When we were still relatively poor, he did notice the rich and their life-styles, but never felt envious of them. Certainly I always had a great confidence in him. You could almost see the electricity flaring around him.

Bruce, by and large, enjoyed the simple, quiet life. "I don't feel like social gatherings," he declared. "Nor am I interested in publicizing myself. But such things are unavoidable in a star's life, particularly in a small place like Hong Kong." What made it worse, he thought, was that there were too many producers trying to be nice to him and he doubted that they were doing it out of friendship. "They think I am only interested in money. That's why they all try to lure me onto their sets by promising me huge sums of nothing else. But at heart I only want a fair share of the profit. What I long for is to make a really good movie." On the whole, we were both satisfied that he had achieved this with *The Way of the Dragon.*

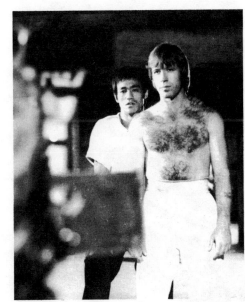

Chuck Norris and Bruce in a scene from The Way of the Dragon.

10

Bruce was never misled by the nature of what had happened to him. His sudden fame and fortune he described as "illusive creations of impostors."

Perhaps the one thing that was most compelling in Bruce's films was his sheer animal magnetism. He had a tremendous energy, some inner force that seemed to grow stronger and more compelling the more he drew on it. He once told Adrian Marshall, "I can feel it sort of bubbling and roaring up inside me."

When *The Way of the Dragon* was in its final stage of production, and everyone was convinced they had a winner, Bruce felt the pressures ease up a bit. In a light mood, he conducted a tour of the studio while a journalist from Singapore interviewed him. She wrote, "It soon becomes obvious that this idol of thousands in Asia is an extremely friendly person. Each of the studio hands we pass by is greeted with a 'good morning' or 'how are you today?' One man thus accosted turned out to be someone else. 'Sorry,' Bruce sings out, 'case of mistaken identity, but good morning all the same.' He makes jokes, massages the neck of a young lady assistant who has a crick in it and admits that he writes his scripts in Chinese first and has somebody else 'polish it up a bit' later as his Chinese is getting a little rusty. He whistles his favorite tune and announces, 'I'd like to teach the world to sing' and then adds, 'But if there's one thing I'm certain of, it is the fact that I can't sing. I tell people I have a rich voice—because it is well off.' He plays tricks with dollar bills. He gives fighting lessons to a few friends, counseling them, 'You must be fierce, but have patience at the same time. Most important of all, you must have complete determination. The worst opponent you can come across is one whose aim has become an obsession. For instance, if a man has decided that he is going to bite off you nose no matter what happens to him in the process, the chances are he will succeed in doing it. He may be severely beaten but that will not stop him carrying out his original objective. That is the real fighter.'

He hurls verbal kicks at gossips—'people in Hong Kong gossip too much.' A photographer arrives to take pictures and asks if Bruce will work for the Shaw Brothers—he tells the man, 'If I have a good script I will consider it. I want to be neutral and act for whichever company can provide me with good scripts. I don't want to be involved in any conflicts or competition here.' Within minutes there are six photographers on the scene, all asking the same question. Irritated, Bruce snaps, 'Tell them I've signed for 20 films with the Shaws.' ''

Later, he revealed something of his dilemma. ''I can usually do what I like in a film. But I also have limitations. People expect me to fight. They expect action. So in a way I am imprisoned by my own success. He talked openly and frankly in a way that may not have endeared him to everyone. He talked about the cultural gap between East and West, criticized production standards in Hong Kong, claimed that too many in the industry were unprofessional. He thought some of the Hong Kong stars misused their considerable power. ''What I detest most is dishonest people who talk more than they are capable of doing. I also find people obnoxious who use false humility as a means to cover their inadequacy.''

Bruce on the set of The Game of Death.

Bruce was never misled by the nature of what had happened to him. His sudden fame and fortune he described as ''illusive creations and imposters'' and he revealed his sincere thoughts in a letter written to his old friend Mito Uyehara, publisher of BLACK BELT:

''After reading your article on me, I have mixed feelings. To many, the word 'success' seems to be a paradise but now that I'm in the midst of it all, it is nothing but circumstances that seem to complicate my innate feelings toward simplicity and privacy. Yet, like it or not, circumstances are thrust upon me and, being a fighter at heart, I sort of fight it in the beginning but soon realize what I need is not inner resistance and needless conflict in the form of dissipation; rather, by joining forces to readjust and make the best of it.

''I can't go wrong because what I've always liked in myself is this 'stickability' toward quality and the sincere desire to do it right. In a way, I am glad that this prosperous happening is occurring to me when I am maturing to a state of readiness and definitely will not blow it because of 'self-glorification' or being 'blinded by illusions.' I am prepared.

''Well, my dear friend—lately friend has come to be a scarce word, a sickening game of watchfulness toward offered friendship—I miss you and our once simple lunches together and our many joyful communications.

''Take care and have fun—hope you are still jogging which is the only form or relaxation to me nowadays.''

Taky Kimura, Bruce's protege in Seattle, went through a severe domestic crisis shortly before Bruce died. At first he had

With his assistant director on the set of The Way of the Dragon.

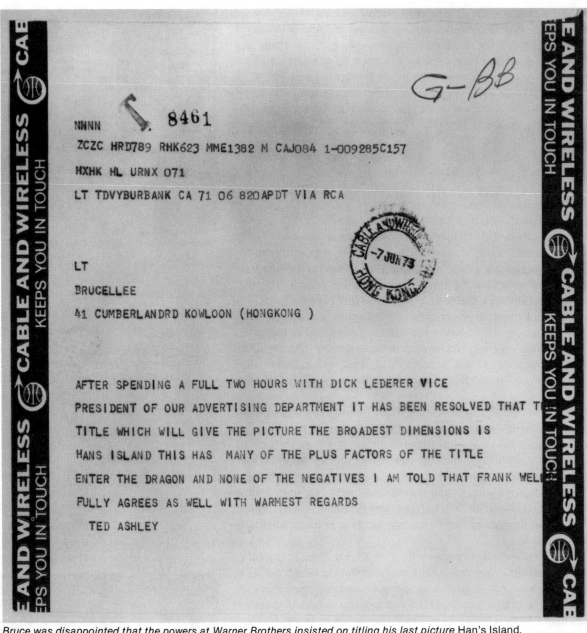

G-BB

NNNN   8461
ZCZC HRD789 RHK623 MME1382 M CAJ084 1-009285C157

HXHK HL URNX 071

LT TDVYBURBANK CA 71 06 820APDT VIA RCA

CABLE AND WIRELESS
-7 JUN 73
HONG KONG

LT

BRUCELLEE

41 CUMBERLANDRD KOWLOON (HONGKONG)

AFTER SPENDING A FULL TWO HOURS WITH DICK LEDERER VICE

PRESIDENT OF OUR ADVERTISING DEPARTMENT IT HAS BEEN RESOLVED THAT T

TITLE WHICH WILL GIVE THE PICTURE THE BROADEST DIMENSIONS IS

HANS ISLAND THIS HAS MANY OF THE PLUS FACTORS OF THE TITLE

ENTER THE DRAGON AND NONE OF THE NEGATIVES I AM TOLD THAT FRANK WELL

FULLY AGREES AS WELL WITH WARMEST REGARDS

   TED ASHLEY

Bruce was disappointed that the powers at Warner Brothers insisted on titling his last picture Han's Island.

NNNN T 312
ZCZC HRB555 RHK783 MMB1369 M CAG331 1-035206C163
HXHK CO URNX 046
TDVYBURBANK CA 46 12 502P PDT VIA RCA

BRUCE LEE
41 CUMBERLANDROAD
TELEPHONE KOWLOON 472-1904
KOWLOONTON (HONGKONG)

DEAR BRUCE
AS REQUESTED WE HAVE GIVEN HE TITLE STILL FURTHER THOUGHT
AND HAVE TAKEN GREATLY INTO ACCOUNT YOUR PREFERENCE AS WELL
THE TITLE WILL THEREFORE BE ENTERED THE DRAGON
LOVE TO YOU AND LINDA
   TED ASHLEY

COL 41 472-1904

Ten days after the previous telegram, Bruce was overjoyed that he had convinced Warner Brothers to retitle the film, Enter the Dragon.

A light moment on the set of Game of Death which Bruce was also writing and directing.

been reluctant to let Bruce know about it—Bruce, after all, was now a great film star and "I didn't want to be known as a hanger-on." To his astonishment, Bruce telephoned him from Hong Kong and chided him. "Look, I'm the same guy I've always been. If there is ever anything you need, just ask me." And he wrote Taky a long letter which Taky says "helped me go through an emotional state successfully." I think letters such as these are sufficient to dispose of at least two falsehoods: that for all his success, Bruce had few friends, and that he tended to forget them. I suppose no one has more than half-a-dozen real friends throughout his or her life and Bruce was more fortunate than most.

It had been Bruce's intention after he had finished *The Way of the Dragon* to take a brief rest and then start work on *The Game of Death*. No script had yet been worked out, but he had a vague idea which would involve bringing some of the world's greatest martial artists and athletes together. Then he heard that his old friend Kareem Abdul-Jabbar was paying a visit to Hong Kong. Bruce called him and suggested that they do a fight scene together, having envisioned that almost nothing could be more intriguing than to see him battling against a man almost two feet taller. Kareem agreed enthusiastically and for a week they planned and then shot some of the most fantastic and beautiful fight scenes ever filmed.

The ending scene of *The Game of Death* was staged in a pagoda, where, on each floor, Bruce met a new opponent. The finale was to be the fight with Kareem. The lead up to this scene was a fight with his good friend and protege, Dan Inosanto. This was a dazzling duel with nunchaku. Dan had introduced Bruce to the nunchaku, and Bruce had mastered them easily as he did most weapons. This fight scene between Dan and Bruce was one of the finest that has ever been staged on film. There was one more fight scene for *Game of Death* between Bruce and a renowned Korean martial artist, but after that the project was tabled for the time being. It was never to be completed in its projected format because of Bruce's death, but in its original form it would have made a spectacular film.

Over the ensuing months, the offers poured in. Run Run Shaw, who only two years earlier had offered Bruce a ridiculously small amount for a film, now offered him a staggering fee, and when Bruce brushed it aside, sent him a signed open contract with a request that he fill in his own figures. Sophia Loren's producer-husband Carlo Ponti was one of the several Italian filmmakers who cabled him fantastic offers, along with scores of other producers from all over the world. As the craze for kung fu movies swept the world, Bruce stood alone at the top of the mountain, unquestionably the hottest property in show business.

"It's like I'm in jail," Bruce said "I'm like a monkey in the zoo. People looking at me and things like that, and basically I like a simple life and I like to joke a lot. But I cannot speak as freely as before because misinterpretation comes in and all kinds of things, you know.

"It hasn't changed me basically, because I know that in my process of being born and going to die something happened which is breaking some records. To me, it doesn't mean anything. It's just something that happens. It's not that I'm proud or better than I ever was, I'm just the same damn old shit."

Whatever he thought he was, he had most assuredly achieved superstardom on the Mandarin circuit, his films having far exceeded the grosses of *The Godfather* and *Sound of Music* in many of the most important areas of the world. Bruce dealt with the flood of offers from an office at the Golden Harvest Studios on Hammer Hill Road, Kowloon, where he kept a seemingly out-of-place pair or old broken spectacles. As he explained to a reporter, "to remind me of the days when I was so broke I couldn't even afford a pair of new glasses."

With rapprochement between China and the United States a new factor in world politics, Bruce realized that his chance of becoming the first Chinese international superstar in history was no longer an impossible dream. The catalyst was Fred Weintraub, formerly vice-president in charge of production for such successes as *Woodstock,* George C. Scott's *Rage* and Jane Fonda's *Klute.* For four years Fred had attempted to put together a martial arts film project, yet had continuosly received a flat no from the major studios. Undeterred, he joined forces with Paul Heller, whose screen credits included Elizabeth Taylor's *Secret Ceremony,* and formed Sequoia Pictures. Shortly thereafter, they commissioned screenwriter Michael Allin to write *Blood and Steel,* which later became *Enter the Dragon.* Warner Brothers contracted to co-produce the film with Concord and Sequoia, agreeing to a budget of U.S. $500,000 (the film eventually cost over $800,000). This was relatively modest by Hollywood standards, but was a huge budget by Mandarin standards. There was no question, either, about who would star. It was a staggering triumph for Bruce.

By February, 1973, Fred Heller, director Robert Clouse, John Saxon, Jim Kelly (the 1971 international middleweight karate champion), actress Ahna Capri, and Bob Wall (who was to play the villainous Oharra) joined Bruce in Hong Kong for ten grueling weeks of filming. Jim Kelly was impressed by the fact that although the Chinese in Hong Kong often had very little money, he found long lines for martial arts films. "No matter what people say, credit for this enormous wave of interest in martial arts movies has to go to Bruce Lee. Bruce is heavy. I've told him personally that I think highly of him for what he is. He's not only good in technique, but he's got a good analytical mind. He analyzes everything he does, and this amazes me. Naturally, I

Bruce and co-stars on the set of Game of Death.

135

Bruce appears to be thinking of something funny in this shot behind the scenes of Enter the Dragon.

have to respect him for being the most successful person that came up through the ranks in the martial arts field.'' On a more personal level Bruce impressed him because "he treats everyone the same, even the kids. Kids in Hong Kong idolize him and I think this is good for them."

Bob Wall explained why he liked the storyline of *Enter the Dragon*. "It was honest and totally believable. More important, it was not detrimental to the martial arts. It's not just another of those eye-for-an-eye stories. Actually Lee is portrayed as a non-violent man. Up to the time he kills Ohara he uses only as much power as necessary for the moment. The theme definitely is in keeping with the principles of martial arts."

Bob was enthusiastic about Bruce's behind-the-scenes role. "He's not only a great martial artist, he's a good actor as well as a good technician. He believes in spontaneity. After instructing us in what to do in the fight scenes, we shot them over and over until he felt it looked very exciting. As a martial artist, it's not fun to be on the receiving end of kicks and punches without being able to retaliate. But working with Bruce taught me to take the punches and kicks without hurting myself and yet make them look authentic. Of course, the fact that Bruce has perfect control of his blows makes it even more reassuring."

It is not easy to detail or chronicle all the pressures that had begun bearing down on Bruce while he was making *Enter the Dragon*, and in the opinion of most of us who were nearest to him, these led to intolerable physical and mental anguish. It was as though he were a high-performance Ferrari which had been driven continuously at redline RPMs and was long overdue for routine maintenance. There were the sheer pressures of living in Hong Kong with its millions of people, high noise level and sweltering humidity. There was the scandal press prying into his privacy, seeking to create sensations of a most sordid kind. There were the producers and entrepreneurs of every type seeking to exploit him and his name. There was the sheer physical and mental strain of making his spectacular films. There were the creative drains on his energies and emotions—how to keep the balance between the demands of international stardom and the need to retain his Mandarin audience. More importantly there was the unpredictable future and the ever-looming question of which path he should take next.

Three incidents that took place during the filming of *Enter the Dragon* are indicative of the added strains. None of them, taken alone, was more than trivial, but collectively, they were extremely nagging setbacks for Bruce. The first was when he severely lacerated his hand during a fight with Bob Wall. Bob explained, "I grabbed a bottle in each hand, smashed off the bottoms and got set. I looked down at the jagged ends—they were lethal weapons all right. I thought, 'My God, they're using real glass!' I looked

Bruce with two cousins on the set. Family members were welcome when Bruce was shooting.

Bruce discusses the script of The Big Boss *with director Lo Wei.*

As on-lookers smile, Bruce plays with an extra on the set of Enter the Dragon.

In a dubbing session. The sound in Mandarin films was dubbed later because of extraneous noise during filming.

In a scene with Kareem Abdul-Jabbar for Game of Death.

across at Bruce. He hadn't flinched. He just quietly said, 'Come ahead, come in at me.' When I took a step I could hear the crunch of the glass grinding underfoot. Then Bruce came flying through the air and kicked me in the upper chest, catapulting me back into a group of extras and the director yelled 'Cut!' ''

All that glass you see shattering at the touch of a finger in Hollywood is imitation glass made of sugar and is harmless. In Hong Kong, however, such sophisticated props are unknown. In choreographing his fight with Bob Wall, Bruce had worked out the moves with meticulous care. Unfortunately, during this particular take, Bruce struck too quickly and Bob had not sufficient time to let go of the bottles. Bruce lunged into the jagged broken glass and blood spurted from the terrible gashes in his hand. It would be a week before he could return to the set. Not only was it painful and inconvenient, but it upset the rhythm of the filming.

In another scene, Bruce has to get past a cobra. To everyone's horror, the cobra struck at Bruce and bit him. Fortunately, the deadly serpent had been devenomized. Nevertheless, its bite resulted in a painful wound, as well as an emotionally unnerving experience.

Adding to all the other pressures was the inevitable challenge from an extra who thought he could ''take'' the master. Bruce had to avoid the streets of Hong Kong more than he would have liked because of this sort of thing. One extra had challenged him while working on *Fist of Fury* and Bruce had toyed with him long enough to convince him that he was wasting his time. On *Enter the Dragon,* there were hundreds of extras, most of them just young kids. One kept constantly challenging Bruce, yelling at him, ''I don't believe you can do everything you say you can.'' Initially Bruce tried to ignore him and to turn the challenge into a jest. Finally, he told the fellow, ''I don't care what you think.''

The kid began to brag that Bruce was afraid to fight him. Bruce put up with it until one day, when all the pressures had put him into a bad mood, he agreed to a match. Bruce struck quickly and the guy went down like a bowling pin. He got up with a bloody lip, only to be knocked down again. Bruce's anger evaporated almost as quickly as it had erupted, and he toyed with the kid until he finally gave up. It was not his intention to physically harm the guy, just to teach him a lesson. As usual, the local newspapers played the story up and according to their version, Bruce had knocked the guy almost unconscious. Some newspapers took a bitter delight in trying to egg Bruce on to fight his various challengers—often condemning him if he didn't. In reality, Bruce could never win and was, in a sense, caught in a trap he couldn't spring. If he accepted a challenge, he seemed a bully. If he refused it, he was made to appear a fake or a wimp. Worst of all, whichever way it went, it was always a good story for the newspapers.

Aside from Bruce, the crew faced some daunting problems in

making the film. No one had really thought ahead to the obstacles likely to be encountered. Although the Americans were more than impressed by the Chinese workers' ability to construct elaborate sets without power tools and other aids taken for granted in Hollywood, the harsh reality was that everything had to be constructed from scratch. Full-scale props, boats, houses were all built by hundreds of Chinese craftsmen and laborers. Then there were the seven fragile praying mantises which had to be flown in from Hawaii for a scene lasting only 20 seconds. Add to that the never-ending language problems which caused delays, as did the vastly different social customs. For example, an assistant prop man forgot to bring a prop one morning and he was so ashamed that he vanished for three days. He had lost face, a serious matter to a Chinese. Some days it took hours just to position the 300 extras and explain what they had to do. Often, after finishing a day with simple explanations of the next day's call sheet, half the extras failed to turn up, and those who did show up often appeared at the wrong times. Faced with the difficulty of finding women to play extra roles, director Robert Clouse hired some of Hong Kong's escort girls for the parts. But they also proved unreliable. Also, people fell sick or got injured. One actor was almost drowned when filming from a junk in the choppy seas. All and all it was anything but an ''easy shoot.''

On the brighter side, director Clouse maintained that Bruce's performance surprised him. ''He's a good actor as well as a supreme martial artist.'' Kurt Hirshler, who edited the film, declared, ''I got a genuine education working with footage of Bruce Lee. He's so lightning-fast and yet everything he does is perfect.'' Although he could slow down the film or stop it as he pleased to observe Bruce's movement, Hirshler added, ''There aren't even signals he gives—not a hint that he's going to throw a punch. He's also in possession of incredible energy. He'd often have to do 10-15 takes of one fight scene, and he'd rarely show any fatigue. I got tired just watching him on film as I edited it.''

Fred Weintraub felt that in many respects they were extremely lucky to finish the film even inside of ten weeks. ''It was completely different from Hollywood. The Chinese say yes to everything, but they don't mean yes. They have no sense of the way we make pictures in Hollywood—their pictures have no continuity and no one cares. Instead of editing, they do their cuts in the camera. They don't bother to fully cover each scene from various angles.'' Moreover, he found it impossible to record sound directly on the set because in all Mandarin movies sound has always been dubbed in afterward. The main reason for this is because of the amount of external noise in the surrounding city. There simply is not enough space in Hong Kong to be able to locate studios in remote areas. In addition, Fred complained, ''It

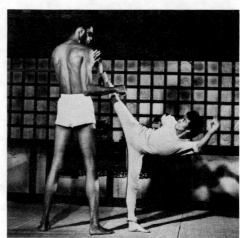

Even with Bruce's great agility, it was impossible to kick Kareem in the face from a standing position.

Bruce makes a point in an interview.

Bruce holds the pair of broken glasses which only two years earlier he could not afford to fix.

Bruce clowns in his office at Golden Harvest Studios with co-star Nora Miao.

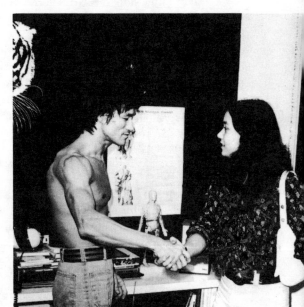

Bruce and I attending a premiere with Raymond Chow.

Bruce in his office at the studio.

Bruce, Brandon, and I appear on Hong Kong TV.

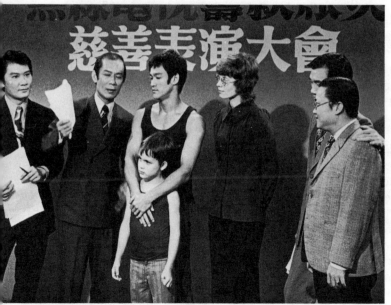

Note the massager he leaned against to relax his injured back.

Bruce uses his telephoto lens on the set of Enter the Dragon. *In his last year he had a keen interest in still photography.*

was impossible to keep the crew and cast quiet during shooting. They just never could understand why they couldn't talk.''

One consequence of Bruce's filming experiences—the humidity, the heat, the constant outpouring of nervous and physical energy, plus the ever-present back pain—was that Bruce was becoming dehydrated and was losing weight at an alarming rate. Bruce was an absolute fanatic about physical fitness, rarely allowing the sun to set without having gone through a thorough workout, but on a physical level Bruce did have his own cross to bear. In truth, Bruce always had a problem with keeping on weight. Even as a child, he was very thin and, apparently, delicate. In fact, when he first returned to Hong Kong from San Francisco, only three months old, the change of climate had a disastrous effect on him and he almost didn't make it.

To some, Bruce's food intake might have seemed adequate, but he burned energy like a furnace. Even as far back in the early years when we lived in Los Angeles, he had developed an interest in health foods and high protein drinks. He also drank a lot of his own juice concoctions made from vegetables and fruits which I prepared in an electric juicer. He took every possible vitamin pill and in time became very knowledgeable about vitamins and very aware of the dangers resulting from excessive dosages.

In Hong Kong, he drank a lot of honey tea and fresh orange juice because he perspired so much, particularly while working. Chinese herbal drinks also formed part of his daily intake. We bought a lot of our food at health stores although it is not true that he refused to eat anything unless it came from one of these. Of course he loved rice and we had it at every meal whether we were having Oriental food or not. He loved Korean and Chinese food, in particular. I remember going out to Korean restaurants in Hong Kong with Jhoon Rhee, and Bruce would sit there and eat and eat, and sweat and sweat and eat and eat—and he just loved it.

There were other problems plaguing Bruce during *Enter the Dragon.* Hong Kong can be a pretty rough place. In addition to people challenging him to fight on the streets, he could never escape from business associates, from people wanting to make deals or thrusting contracts under his nose, from the press and electronic media, from autograph hunters mobbing him whenever he appeared. In Hollywood, it would have been relatively easy to get out of town on weekends or relax for a day or two in the country, but in cramped Hong Kong this was totally out of the question. On the other hand, by nature and temperament, Bruce did everything in high gear. Recall that when he was a child, his family had nicknamed him (in Chinese) ''Never sits still.'' As a result, although he knew he needed to relax, somehow there was always something that he honestly felt had to be attended to immediately. Throughout early 1973, Bruce was con-

144

Raymond Chow on my right, with Alex Rose and Fred Weintraub. Fred co-produced Enter the Dragon.

Dan Inosanto squares off with Bruce in a nunchaku battle for Game of Death.

stantly on the go, discussing scripts or talking for hours on the telephone or holding conferences. Toward the end he had so many problems in his head that he could not sleep. Oftentimes during his waking hours he was especially moody.

I tried to tell him that there was no longer any need for him to work so hard, that his career was now running along the right lines and the future was assured. Besides, I emphasized, the important thing that the four of us should be together, that as long as we had each other, everything was fine. Yet it was not easy for Bruce to forget the relatively lean times we had experienced in our early years, and he was determined that the children and I should never again have to face financial uncertainty. It was his goal in life, even beyond making the best quality films and being the best martial artist he could be, to provide well for his family. I don't know if that characteristic can be attributed to his Asian heritage or to his own personality, probably a combination of the two, but it was certainly an overriding concern. It must also be remembered that at this point in time, proceeds for *Way* were just beginning to trickle in (to pay bills we had already incurred), and *Enter the Dragon* had not yet been released. *Enter the Dragon* was a large gamble, for both Bruce and the American producers—would Western audiences take to this sort of action picture? Would they accept a Chinese hero? Would Hong Kong moviegoers be turned off by the "Western" approach to this film? These were all unanswered questions.

Bruce's future depended on the success of *Enter the Dragon*. He had visions of leaving Hong Kong and returning to the United States where he could truly carry out his dreams of being an international star and provide better living conditions and educational opportunities for his children. Whether or not this would be possible all rode on the reception of *Dragon*. It was an extremely tenuous time. On a couple of occasions when his energy and mood levels were low, Bruce would talk about "in case anything happens to me" for he was aware that everything depended on a fragile foundation—his continued physical fitness. It used to scare me when he talked like this because I had great faith in his abilities beyond just his fighting techniques. He was an accomplished actor and was beginning to develop his writing and directorial skills. I had no doubt that his career could expand in these directions if and when he chose to ease himself out of the action roles that the public savored. But he was right in knowing that, at least for the time being, his future depended upon his physical prowess.

11

Fred Weintraub had known Bruce for some time, even before we lived in Hong Kong. He recalls, "I knew Bruce as a very quiet and considerate person. I remember on my birthday once, Bruce drove all the way down to Chinatown to buy me a set of nunchaku. I found him interesting—indeed, everyone was fascinated by his martial arts skill. Linda was very different, however—quiet but firm. Bruce was a really nice guy at that time." Near the end, however, Fred began to see a major change in his dear friend. "Bruce was undoubtedly nervous, even apprehensive, about *Enter the Dragon*. A lot was riding on it—it was his first big international film. Then, of course, he was on his home ground and I think he wanted to avoid giving the impression of partiality toward Americans by favoring them at the expense of his own ethnic group. So there was this dichotomy operating for him. And on the whole, he wanted the film to be more Chinese than American, which was very understandable.

"About our differences—well, first, the script could never have been to his liking," Fred explained. "He and the writer just didn't see eye-to-eye. It took us two to three weeks before Bruce finally showed up. Meanwhile, I'm getting these hysterical cables from Warner Brothers—where's Bruce? So I just went ahead and shot sequences, even though Bruce wasn't ready to start. I kept telling Warner Brothers he was going to show up every day—for Linda had told me that eventually he would. Eventually he did show up. I found him very different from the guy I'd known in Los Angeles. And the first thing that happened was that he walked

James Coburn says that, "Toward the end of his life, Bruce seemed to be carrying a great weight . . . something had set in. He was being hit on all sides by everybody . . . and he had to have his guard up all the time."

147

Bruce poses with two popular Hong Kong entertainers.

John Saxon and director Bob Clouse confer with Bruce on the set of Enter the Dragon.

A scene from Enter the Dragon.

off the set on the very first day. This was after he had had an argument with Raymond Chow. The film was supposed to be a joint production between Concord (Bruce and Raymond's company), Sequoia (Weintraub and Heller's company), and Warner Brothers. The newspaper called it a Golden Harvest Production, exclusively, so Bruce called Raymond Chow and then walked off.''

When Bruce arrived home he expressed to me his utter frustration. What was of vital importance to him was to maintain a high level of creative control throughout the filming, of *Enter the Dragon*. The fact that Raymond Chow had marketed the film as a Golden Harvest production implied that Raymond had intentions of standing at the foot of the helm from day one. In a sense he was testing Bruce who, as it turned out, was not in the least bit inclined to give an inch on this most crucial issue. And so Bruce made a point of it and everyone respected him for it. After all, it was his first international film and for all intents and purposes it was Bruce's career on the chopping block, not Raymond's.

"I think he was kinda hibernating in those first few weeks. I think he was terribly frightened,'' insists Fred. "Here he had this big chance—and there's no question that he would have been the biggest superstar if he had lived, for he had this thing that happens to great performers on screen—it's a kind of magnetism. It's the same with guys like Clint Eastwood—just a nice guy when you meet him at a party but something unique and special when he gets on the screen. Throughout the picture about the only two people Bruce would talk to were Bob Clouse and Linda. I tried to keep the whole thing on a strictly producer/star footing.

"He was nervous the first day we actually started shooting. You could see him twitching. Bob said to me, 'He's twitching.' The first scene with him was a very simple one but it took 20 takes. Once Bruce finally got rolling, however, and he began to work with Bob Clouse, whom he respected, he was truly professional in every sense of the word—really magnificent.

"But there were real nervous worries before we got him to that point. Warner Brothers kept sending all these rewritten versions of *Enter the Dragon*, hoping we'd get one that Bruce would like. There we were—12 days into the picture and yet another script arrived from Hollywood. I rang them and said 'I've had enough—I'm on my way home.' Then Linda called and said, 'It's going to be all right tomorrow.' And it was.

"It was not easy for him—and I don't think anybody can be glib about it. You can't dismiss it as ego-tripping or anything like that. Here he was, the greatest martial artist-actor of them all, lining up, as it were, for the Olympics. It was the big moment—all he had been striving for. I got the impression that somewhere or other along the line in the U.S. Bruce felt he had been shunted— that the guys like Coburn and McQueen considered him as a teacher, but never considered him as a major screen personality, and suddenly here he had his chance to outshine them all. He wanted to prove he had been right. That he wasn't a crazy man.

"Remember that it was extremely rare for a Chinese to be given star billing in an American film. Everything was riding on it. And somewhere in the middle of it all, there were these people talking about 'foreign devils'—there was a lot of talk by the Chinese, a lot of anti-Americanism—here were the 'foreign devils' horning in on a Chinese art. So when he got his hand hurt, he felt it was a sort of portent."

Bruce died before *Enter the Dragon* was ever released. The picture had gone way over budget, but when Warner Brothers first saw it, they knew they had a winner and authorized an additional $50,000 for special music and sound effects.

On the set of Enter the Dragon, *Bruce makes a point with director Bob Clouse and producer Fred Weintraub.*

"Bruce had no real idea, I think, of just how big the picture was going to be," Fred continued. "Certainly it surprised Warner Brothers. I think it's going to be a classic film—and I've advised against ever releasing it on television. I think it will come back every three or four years for the rest of time, because Bruce is no longer with us and if you want to see him, then you've got to see his films. There's a whole cult growing up around him—and I think it will grow bigger rather than die away. It won't date the way the Bond films have—because Bruce's films didn't rely on scientific gadgetry, which will date. Think of it—it broke all records in Japan, which is traditionally the worst market in the world for Chinese films. Most Chinese films are anti-Japanese and everybody felt the Japanese would reciprocate—but they didn't. I believe Bruce would have earned a million dollars on his next picture—on his salary alone. He was pure dynamite. He was an 'exploitation star' the way John Wayne, Clint Eastwood, and Cary Grant in their own milieu were. He would have been very strong. He was a very lonely guy, however, and he always kept you a little at arm's length—you were always one step away from meeting the real Bruce Lee, but, in a funny way, that's the quality that makes a star. I mean all that intensity that was part of his personality, it came through on the screen. He could have done a great love story in my opinion. Because he had so much inside him, it was just a question of giving it out. Off screen, certainly he'd take off his shirt and show you his muscles and all that—he'd show his punching and so on, but in Hong Kong at that time, toward the end, he never gave you as much in person as he was capable of giving. The only time you saw the real man I think, was when you saw him playing with his kids. Everything would change then, everything would be different. And except for Linda he trusted nobody in this world. Linda was the only one he would talk to, or trust, or have confidence in—she was everything to Bruce."

There are contradictions in how various people viewed Bruce

149

Bruce poses in traditional Mandarin-period film garb.

during this period. Fred Weintraub says Bruce was a changed person from the man he had known in Los Angeles, that he was no longer friendly and kept others at a distance. Taky Kimura and Dan Inosanto, among others, have commented that Bruce was the same tried and true friend that they had always known. The truth, of course, lies somewhere in between. The working and living conditions in Hong Kong were not ideal, and there were a lot of new things happening to Bruce to upset his inner harmony. Some people might have gotten the impression that he was closing himself off, but in my opinion, he was using the quiet time he had, when he was not filming or making appearances, to balance himself, to reorder his internal universe.

By nature, Bruce and I were quite different in some ways. I was the yin to his yang, generally quieter and calmer. I could sometimes straighten out minor hassles for Bruce which would cause him no end of frustration. It seemed only natural that I should occasionally run interference for him so that he could devote his time to his work. We were very close during the years of struggle as couples tend to be when there are difficult times. They were not the best of times, but we were a solid force.

I would like to be able to write that Bruce's last days were among his happiest but, regrettably, this would not be wholly true. The nature of the motion picture industry often brings out the very worst in people. With such enormous sums of money at stake, there are wheels within wheels. As in every business, too, there are personality clashes due to temperament and behavior. For a long time, since his first film in Bangkok, Bruce and Lo Wei, the director, had been on anything but good terms. Bruce thought the director too conceited and selfish and a man who simply wanted to use people. On one particular day, Bruce was at the Golden Harvest studios, discussing ideas for *The Game of Death* with Raymond Chow when he heard that Lo Wei was in the screening room down the hall. To Bruce the name summed up almost everything that was wrong with Mandarin films. Bruce's patience had been exhausted earlier that day, in essence it was the straw that broke the camel's back, and so he rushed down to the screening room and in a loud voice let Lo Wei know what he thought of him.

Satisfied at having given vent to his feelings, he returned to Raymond Chow's office. At this stage, the incident seemed at an end, but then Lo Wei's wife appeared and tempers again became heated. As one can imagine, by this time a considerable crowd had gathered. Mrs. Lo went back to her husband, leaving Bruce boiling over with anger and frustration. Under normal circumstances, he would have quickly calmed down. Instead, he charged back to the screening room and gave Lo Wei another piece of his mind. When in the midst of it all the director suddenly accused Bruce of threatening him physically, the police were called. And as usual, no sooner did the police arrive, than a swarm of reporters followed. Lo Wei demanded that Bruce sign a paper promising not to harm him physically. Bruce, annoyed and upset by the whole incident and anxious to get the reporters off the premises, agreed to sign. Later he could have kicked himself, for the signing of the document obviously incriminated him.

Bruce had a previous engagement to appear on Hong Kong TV that evening and the matter was raised again. Throughout his life Bruce had never feared to state openly and frankly how he felt about people or problems. This particular evening was no different and in the ensuing discussion he did not conceal his dislike of the director or his methods. In an attempt to show how absurd were suggestions that he had physically threatened Lo Wei, Bruce decided to demonstrate a simple shoulder push on the interviewer, who was quite agreeable. Unfortunately, the next morning papers, still seeking for sensation, built the incident up into more headlines. I only relate this story about Lo Wei as an example of the kinds of incidents which were cluttering up Bruce's life. That incident in itself was not such a big deal, but the treatment of it by the press blew it up out of proportion. It was my observation of the press surrounding Bruce that they often became obsessive in their zeal to sell newspapers, and the truth was that, as is the case with any major star, the most trivial events often resulted in headlines.

Adrian Marshall says, ''I think we've got to see Bruce's occasional anger as all part of the creative and artistic temperament. I mean, I don't think Bruce liked being mad. But it was simply part of his vitality. Mostly, Bruce was a very courteous man, although he never believed in pulling his punches. He was not going to be fooled or put upon by anybody. And he got away with things that no man who didn't have his charm could have ever done. For instance, he could put you down, and you wouldn't feel the slightest degree of offense. He didn't mean to be offensive and, unless you were a fool, you didn't take it that way. But if he put you through it on occasions, he always wanted to help you up again—he wanted you to gain something from the experience. He would say 'Turn the stumbling block into an stepping stone.' Whenever something went wrong or you found yourself up against a difficulty, he tried to turn the problem into something of a positive, rather than a negative nature. 'This is good, because now you realize that you can overcome that, and I can guarantee you that you will.' And nine times out of ten, you did. Mind you, it didn't always work—but it worked for him, but no doubt that was because he had talent.''

Our world was severely shaken on the afternoon of May 10, 1973. Bruce was working at the Golden Harvest studios, dubbing the sound to the final print of *Enter the Dragon*. Although it was an intensely hot and humid day, it was necessary to shut down

Bruce demonstrates a move with John Saxon on the set of Enter the Dragon.

Bruce on the phone in his office.

Brandon attends a function with his dad.

the noisy air conditioning unit in order to prevent extraneous noise from finding its way onto the sound track. Bruce, for all the care he took to remain physically fit, was for once physically exhausted and mentally weary. Although the people with him thought he looked unusually tired, in view of the energies he had expended in his recent film fights and the intensity of the heat, they paid little attention to him when he excused himself and walked to a nearby vacant rest room where he collapsed on the floor. He told me later that, to the best of his knowledge, he did not lose consciousness, for he remembers hearing approaching footsteps and groping around on the floor, pretending that he had dropped his glasses. Upon returning to the dubbing room he was scarcely in the door when he collapsed and lost consciousness. Then he vomited and had an attack of convulsions.

One of the dubbing crew ran to Raymond Chow's office and alerted him that Bruce was ill. Chow asked someone to call a doctor and rushed over to the dubbing room where, according to his testimony before a coroner's jury a few months later, he found Bruce "having difficulty in breathing. He was making a loud noise and was shaking." By this time, one of the women at the studio had telephoned me. "Bruce is sick and they're taking him to the hospital," she said.

"What's the matter?" I questioned with a note of urgency.

"Oh I think it's a stomach upset," she replied.

This phone conversation did not imply an emergency situation. It is not uncommon in Hong Kong for people to go to the hospital for relatively minor problems. And especially with someone like Bruce, if he had the slightest medical disability, they would rush him to the hospital. I thought at worst it might be his appendix, or perhaps a hernia, which he'd had before. In this frame of mind, I set off for the hosptial. I was not prepared for what I would find when I got there.

On arriving at the hospital, according to Dr. Langford, Bruce made "breathing noises," which stopped and were followed by a series of convulsions. Three other doctors were summoned, including a neurosurgeon, Dr. Peter Woo. Bruce was also suffering from an extremely high fever and his body was bathed in sweat. Soon he began to gasp and his every breath seemed as if it were his last. Now and again his eyes opened but they were not focusing. I asked Dr. Langford if he was going to be all right. "He's very sick," he replied.

At this stage, Dr. Langford was prepared to do a tracheotomy if Bruce stopped breathing. The convulsions continued, his entire body being involved in this motion, his arms giving the doctors considerable trouble because, as Dr. Langford testified, "he was very strong and difficult to control." When Bruce failed to respond after a while, the neurosurgeon examined him and surmised that there was something wrong with Bruce's brain. "We gave him a drug (Manitol) to reduce the swelling of the brain which we had detected," said Dr. Langford. The doctors were prepared for surgery at this stage if the Manitol didn't work but, after a couple of hours, Bruce began to regain consciousness. "It was quite dramatic," Dr. Langford told the jury. "First he was able to move a bit, then he opened his eyes, then he made a sign, but could not speak. He recognized his wife and made signs of recognition but could not talk. Later he was able to speak but it was slurred, different from the usual way he talked. By the time he was transferred to another hospital, he was able to remember aloud and joke." Dr. Woo said a blood test had shown a possible malfunction of the kidney. Asked if the symptoms were such as could occur in a person suffering from overwork and exhaustion, Dr. Langford replied, "No." He also said that Bruce had seemed near to death. Bruce was quickly transferred to St. Theresa's Hospital where the facilities were better.

Almost the first words Bruce said to me after he regained consciousness were that he had, in fact, felt very close to death—but that he could still exert his will and he had told himself "I'm going to fight it—I'm going to make it—I'm not going to give up" because he knew that if he thought any other way, he would die. I believe he sensed it himself, not simply that he would die, but that a major turning point was imminent. He loved the song "And When I die," specifically the part that says if it's peace you find in dying, then let the time be near. Once or twice he mentioned, "Maybe that's the only place where I'll find peace."

John Saxon, who starred with him in *Enter the Dragon*, says that Bruce was really shaken by his collapse in May and said to him, "Maybe if my tests don't work out, there isn't going to be a Bruce Lee." When I heard Bruce talk like this, it genuinely frightened me.

A week later we flew to Los Angeles where a team led by Dr. David Reisbord conducted a brain scan and brain flow study, as well as a complete physical and electroencephalogram. They found no abnormality in his brain functions, in fact, they found absolutely nothing wrong with his entire body. Indeed they told him he had the body of an 18-year-old. As to Bruce's earlier collapse on May 10, Dr. Langford told me Bruce had suffered a cerebral edema, which is the excessive collecting of fluid surrounding the brain, and that he had further suffered *grand mal*—idiopathic—which means a type of convulsion due to no known primary cause. The standard treatment for this is to prescribe medication, which calms brain activity. Bruce was prescribed the drug Dilantin, but, inexplicably, no traces of this were found in his body after death.

I should say here that none of Bruce's family ever suffered from epilepsy, even in a mild form, and that Bruce had never suffered from it either. The doctors told me that convulsions similar

Bruce and Brandon with Bruce's mother, Grace.

Bruce plays around wearing a fur coat in Hong Kong's sweltering summer humidity.

153

Bruce returned to visit his family home on Nathan Road in Kowloon in the summer of 1970.

Brandon, Grandma Lee, and friend.

to epileptic seizures can be caused by lack of sugar in the blood, lack of oxygen, uremia, injury to the brain from an accident, brain tumors or meningitis. True epilepsy, however, shows no such antecedents—it just happens and, although it is apparently the result of something wrong with the chemistry of the brain, what this something is is not known. Dr. Reisbord told me that at no time had Bruce suffered from epilepsy. Indeed, it is clear that he suffered a cerebral edema, but what caused it remains unknown.

While in Los Angeles, Bruce agreed to return to the States in August to help promote *Enter the Dragon* and to appear on a series of promotions including *The Johnny Carson Show*. We returned to Hong Kong with a clean bill of health and renewed energy. Bruce was optimistic about the future and looking forward to slaying more dragons. Little did I know or even suspect that my Little Dragon had less than three months to live.

It was about this time that Bruce decided that we would return to live in the United States where life was easier and there were more opportunities. He would return perhaps twice a year to Hong Kong to make a picture because there he would be afforded the added control and freedom necessary to pursue specialized film projects. Above all else, however, the whole direction of his life was toward improving the quality of his work. He wanted to educate the audience through the medium of film. He wanted them to understand that there was far more to the martial arts than just plain fighting. In honest pursuit of this main goal, he was shrewd enough to know when and where to seek out people of true integrity. Ted Ashley, chairman of the board of Warner Brothers, had been a friend of long standing, so just before *Enter the Dragon* was to be released, Bruce wrote the following heartfelt letter:

Ted, nowadays, my offers for doing a film have reached a point which I guarantee you will both surprise as well as shock you. Viewing from the angle of efficient practical business sense, I hope we will be fair and square and have mutual trust and confidence—I have had a bad experience doing a picture with some person or organization in Hong Kong. In other words, I was burned once, and didn't like it.

Without Bruce Lee, I am sure that Warner Brothers will definitely and factually suffer no loss, and vice versa; therefore, and I sincerely mean it, that is from one human being to another, practical business or whatever it is, I sincerely hope that during this meeting I will find a genuine and truthful friend, Ted Ashley.

As a friend, I am sure you agree with me that, after all, quality, extremely hard work and professionalism are what cinema is all about. My 20 years of experience, both in martial arts and acting, has apparently led to the successful harmony of appropriateness of showmanship and genuine, efficient, artful expression. In short, this is it and ain't nobody knows it like I know it. Pardon my bluntness, but that is me!

Under such circumstances, I sincerely hope that you will open up the genuineness within you and be absolutely fair and square in our transactions. Because of our friendship, I am holding up my money-making time—like ten offers from hungry producers—to look forward to this meeting. You see, Ted, my obsession is to make, pardon the expression, the fuckingest action motion picture that has ever been made.

In closing, I will give you my heart, but please do not give me your head only; in return, I Bruce Lee will always feel the deepest appreciation for the intensity of your involvement.

Bruce saw little long-term future for kung fu films. In fact, he predicted that the craze for them would not last beyond three years. In regard to his own career, he had already branched out, quite successfully, into writing, producing and directing and had fully intended to continue along these lines. For the moment, however, while he awaited the release of *Enter the Dragon*, he worked on the *The Game of Death* script and considered the flood of other film offers. At times, I tried to talk him into easing up a little, but he would cut me short by saying, "The biggest detriment to relaxation is to say: I must relax." I don't think he would have felt right if he had taken time off to go on a trip or something like that. In fact, I believe it would have been useless to try. By this stage, he had convinced himself that he was relaxing when he was working, and I believe that his mind would have been too preoccupied by his work for him to have enjoyed himself doing anything else. I know actor John Saxon took the view that Bruce's life was just "spiraling away." He was involved in such a whirlwind of activity that the goals he originally set out to achieve were rapidly being replaced by even higher goals.

Bruce made two contradictory statements in the last months of his life. He said, "There's no limit, no end in sight, to how far I can ascend in my knowledge of film and the martial arts." while at the same time he told me, "I don't know how much longer I can keep this up." The intense strain and mood swings were certainly there. I was aware of the immensity of my husband's difficulties and did my best to support him. This was a time of change for Bruce and our life-style, but, as he often told me "to change with change is the changeless state," by which he meant that the rhythm of his life could not be broken if he kept pace with the changes happening around him.

Bruce and his mother, Grace.

Three generations.

155

12

And finally the words of Jhoon Rhee: "Bruce was a man of victory."

It was around noon on July 20, 1973, and I was preparing to leave our Kowloon house to lunch with a girlfriend. Bruce was in his study, which was the most important room in the house. It was here he kept his magnificent library, amounting to several thousand books dealing with every conceivable aspect of physical combat, ancient and modern, as well as weapons of all kinds, calisthenics, sports, filmmaking and both Eastern and Western philosophy. Bruce practically lived in his study, and would often remain there working at his desk into the dead of night. Through the balcony window he could see our garden which had been laid out in the Japanese style, including a goldfish pond with a little bridge across it and a stream which meandered in and out of the trees and through the Korean grass. By Hong Kong standards we had a lavish home—a large house with spacious grounds surrounded by an eight-foot-high stone wall and a large wrought-iron gate at the main entrance. We had been lucky to find a residential property available. Living in the small flat on Waterloo Hill had been difficult for Bruce because he could not have his separate study or set up his library and workout equipment. It was like living in any congested city, except in addition to that, there was the noise of daily communication and the constant clacking of mah-jong tiles at night.

Bruce told me that Raymond Chow was due to come over that afternoon to talk about the script ideas for *The Game of Death*, and that they would probably dine later with George Lazenby, the actor who took over the James Bond role between Sean Connery and Roger Moore. Raymond hoped Lazenby would co-star in the film. Bruce was his usual industrious self when I left him. That was the last conversation I ever had with my husband.

Raymond Chow arrived around 2:00 p.m. and he and Bruce

worked together until around 4:00 p.m. After that, they drove to the home of Betty Ting-pei, an actress from Taiwan, who was also to have a leading role in the film.

At Betty's flat, Bruce appeared quite normal. They went over the script together, working out more details. Raymond eventually left to prepare for the dinner meeting with George Lazenby. A short time later Bruce complained of a headache, and Betty gave him a tablet of Equagesic—a kind of super aspirin which had been prescribed for her by her personal physician. Apart from that, Bruce took nothing but a couple of soft drinks. Around 7:30 p.m. Bruce said he didn't feel well and went to lie down in a bedroom, and was still asleep when Raymond phoned to find out why they were late for dinner. Betty said that she could not awaken Bruce.

Raymond returned to her apartment. So far as Raymond could tell, Bruce was still asleep and he saw no signs of anything out of the ordinary. When he tried to awaken him, there was again no response. He ordered Betty to call a doctor, who came immediately. He, too, found Bruce lying peacefully on the bed. The doctor later testified that he spent ten minutes trying to revive Bruce and then had him rushed to the Queen Elizabeth Hospital.

I returned home about four o'clock and spent the evening exercising and watching TV in Bruce's study with our two children, Brandon and Shannon. I remember thinking it a little unusual that Bruce hadn't phoned, for although he had told me he would probably be dining out, he usually called to confirm arrangements. Instead, sometime around ten o'clock Raymond Chow called. There was a note of urgency in his voice.

"Would you go to the Queen Elizabeth Hospital right away, Linda. Bruce is on the way there—in an ambulance."

"What's the matter?," I demanded.

"I don't know—something like last time."

Instantly I was alarmed. The memory of Bruce's collapse on May 10th was still all too fresh in my mind.

I arrived at the hospital about 15 minutes before the ambulance, but at first it seemed as if there had been some mistake. When I inquired about Bruce, the man at the desk suggested, "Somebody must have been joking—we don't know anything about it." This didn't seem completely implausible, since many extraordinary events characterized our lives in Hong Kong. I had thought it was Raymond's voice on the phone, but perhaps I was being fooled. I was within seconds of calling home where I fully expected Bruce to be, wondering where I was. Then the ambulance arrived. Bruce was apparently unconscious but I could not find out exactly what was happening because the doctors were swarming around him. He was wheeled into an emergency ward where a team began massaging his heart. It never occurred to me that he might die, let alone that he might already be dead.

Actor Bruce Lee Dies In Hong Kong Hospital

HONG KONG — (UPI) — Bruce Lee, a one-time University of Washington student who parlayed his knowledge of Oriental martial arts into a movie career, died last night at Queen Elizabeth Hospital. He was 32.

The government information service said the cause of Lee's death was not immediately determined. He died shortly after admission to the hospital.

Lee starred in numerous films made here featuring use of karate, Kung-fu and other martial arts. The films recently became popular internationally, particularly in the United States.

In Hollywood, Warner Bros. said Lee was born in San Francisco in 1940 of Chinese parents, raised in Hong Kong and attended University of Washington, where he majored in philosophy.

Lee then moved to Los Angeles with his wife, Linda, and appeared in a number of television roles.

Lee returned to Hong Kong where producer Raymond Chow starred him in

BRUCE LEE
Karate and films

"Fists of Fury," "The Big Boss" and "The Chinese Connection," all featuring karate. The films were made in Mandarin and dubbed in English. A film, "Enter the Dragon," was made in English last spring and is scheduled for release in August by Warner Bros.

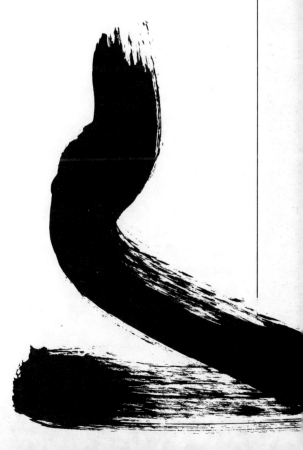

Rites held for kung-fu idol

James Coburn, left, and Steve McQueen, right, were two of the six pallbearers who helped carry Bruce Lee's casket from the chapel at the Butterworth mortuary, 300 E. Pine St., to a waiting hearse. A representative from the funeral home, in the middle, directed the pallbearers.

Bruce had talked about death more than once in recent months. He was convinced that he would never live to be an old man, nor, indeed did he want to. He frequently told people in his last days that he hated the idea of growing old and weak.

"I won't live as long as you," he told me one day.

"Why would you think that?" I asked. "You're a lot healthier than I am and in far better condition, for heaven's sake."

"I don't really know. The fact is I don't know how long I can keep this up." This was one of his many moods at this point in his life.

And so now, for the second time within three months, I found myself in a bare hospital emergency room, watching a team of doctors working on my husband. Strangely, I felt almost no emotion. I suppose I was too numbed by shock. Grief, despair, and the sense of loss—all these were to come later. Besides, I believed Bruce was merely unconscious for nobody had told me he was already dead. After a minute or so, they suddenly rushed Bruce upstairs and we all had to run along a corridor to an intensive care unit. Here they injected drugs directly into Bruce's heart and applied electric shock. Somebody tried to pull me away saying, "I don't think you want to see this," but I struggled free and insisted, "Leave me alone—I want to know what's happening." Then I noticed that the EKG machine recording Bruce's heartbeat was emitting a "flat-line" indicating Bruce's heart had stopped beating. I suddenly realized what had really happened. Yet, I still refused to believe the unbelievable. I was convinced that Bruce would always pull through. He had so much life and vitality, so much inner force. And he had such control over his mind and his body. Throughout his life, he had fought his way out of so many adverse situations and survived so much. I simply could not accept the idea that he would not survive as he had previously on May 10th. When I asked the doctor, I did not use the word dead. It was not a word I could use about Bruce. Instead I asked, "Is he alive?" The doctor shook his head.

When the doctors left Bruce's side I stayed with him to assure myself that there *really* was nothing I could do. It was at this point, when his life force was barely extinguished that I felt an incredible strength surge through my body and spirit. I remember Raymond Chow telephoning his wife, asking her to come and pick us up. I remember the head of the medical team asking me if I wanted an autopsy and replying, "Yes, I want to know why he died." I remember the flash of photographers' bulbs and the reporters swarming into the hospital. No panic or despair. The determination and courage of Bruce himself passed to me. In a flash I knew what lay ahead and how I should deal with everything in the best possible way for Bruce, Brandon and Shannon.

Once the news of Bruce's death broke, of course, the Hong

Kong press went wild. I could understand the furor. The death of any superstar is newsworthy. Had he been a man given to bad habits, had he been killed like James Dean in a road accident—even then, I suppose, there would have been much speculation. But that a man of Bruce's astonishing vitality, energy and sheer physical fitness should suddenly be snuffed out like a candle at the young age of 32—perhaps people cannot be blamed for hypothesizing.

The day after Bruce's death, Raymond Chow appeared on Hong Kong television to talk about it. Part of the resulting confusion was my fault. Raymond had asked if I objected to him making it clear that Bruce had died at home rather than at Betty's house. I said it didn't matter to me—he could do as he thought best. We both sensed that the headlines would be larger and more dramatic if the press could link Bruce's name with Betty's. But I really didn't care then and I don't care now—it didn't seem to me all that important. I was preoccupied with the funeral arrangements and thoughts of my children at the time. Raymond did not specifically say that Bruce had died at home, but he implied that he had. When the press found out the truth, it seemed that Raymond had been lying. And if he had been lying, then why? As a result, the wildest theories and rumors suddenly began to fly in all directions.

The release of the autopsy report did nothing to lessen the sensation of Bruce's death. Traces of cannabis or marijuana were found in Bruce's stomach. The newspapers immediately went to town on the idea that Bruce was a drug addict and had taken drugs to help boost his extraordinary feats. In sharp contrast, all the medical evidence given at the coroner's inquiry disclosed that there was no possibility that cannabis could have caused his death. One doctor said that the cannabis was no more significant than if Bruce had drunk a cup of tea.

The greatest care was taken to get the true reason for Bruce's death. A doctor in the forensic division of the Hong Kong government laboratory examined the contents of Bruce's stomach and interior organs and other samples were sent to Australia and New Zealand. The only "foreign" substance found in Bruce's organs was the Equagesic.

Dr. R. R. Lycette of Queen Elizabeth Hospital viewed Bruce's death as a hypersensitivity to one or more of the compounds in the tablet Equagesic. Some people, for instance, are allergic to penicillin, and the suggestion was that Bruce, in some chemical way, was hypersensitive to those ingredients. Dr. Lycette also said he had examined Bruce's skull but had found no injuries on it. Bruce's brain, however, was "swollen like a sponge," weighing 1,575 grams against a normal 1,400 grams. But the trouble could not have been a brain hemorrhage because none of the vessels in the brain were blocked or broken. Dr. Lycette said

Mrs. Linda Lee, wife of Bruce Lee, kung-fu movie idol, walked with the couple's daughter, Shannon, 6, to a limousine after yesterday's burial at Lake View Cemetery. The 32-year-old actor died July 20. An unidentified man was alongside Mrs. Lee. Another child, Brandon, 8, also survives.—Staff photos by Jerry Gay. (Details, A 16.)

that the brain swelling could have taken place either in half a minute or half a day.

The cannabis theory was completely thrown out by Professor R. D. Teare, professor of forensic medicine at the University of London—and the top expert in the case. He had overseen more than 90,000 autopsies and declared that to ascribe the cause of death to cannabis would be irrational. He decided that the edema had been caused by hypersensitivity to either meprobamate or aspirin, or a combination of the two; both are present in Equagesic. However unusual this might be—and cases were rare—this was the only feasible solution. The view was accepted by the jury and a verdict of "misadventure" returned. After the verdict, the reporters rushed at me, demanding to know if I was satisfied. I could only reply "Well, it doesn't really change anything, does it?"

Bruce had two funeral ceremonies, one in Hong Kong and the other in Seattle, where he lies buried. The first was for his friends and fans in Hong Kong, the second was a more private ceremony.

I decided that Bruce would like to be buried in the Chinese outfit he had worn in *Enter the Dragon*. He often wore it at home just because it was very comfortable. I attended the funeral at the Kowloon Funeral Parlor wearing all white, the Chinese color for mourning. The casket was not present at the start of the ceremonies, but each person upon entering the room walked up to a kind of altar where Bruce's picture was displayed with ribbons and flowers decorating the area and a Chinese banner saying "A Star Sinks in the Sea of Art." Three long incense sticks and two candles also burned in front of his picture. After each person had bowed three times, he or she walked back and took a seat in the main hall. When Brandon and Shannon arrived wearing burlap robes and white hoods, we sat down on cushions on the floor. The Chinese band played a traditional funeral song which sounds like "Auld Lang Syne." In addition to Bruce's many relatives, scores of his close friends and famous stars and movie personalties were in attendance. Outside, the streets and multistoried balconies and rooftops were lined with people as far as the eye could see. Later I heard that people had been injured in the pushing and shoving mob of approximately 25,000 people. Eventually, Bruce's casket was brought into the room and positioned near the altar and people filed past the open coffin to see him for the last time, his body covered with glass to prevent anyone from touching him.

I had decided to bury Bruce in the peace and calm of Seattle where the light rain that he loved so much falls often and there are lakes and mountains and trees all around. I think his happiest times were spent in Seattle, and I intended to return there with my children to live. I was concerned, too, because the political future of Hong Kong is uncertain and I decided that the day might

Bruce's funeral in Hong Kong was a Buddhist ceremony. In this photo I am wearing the traditional white mourning dress.

My friend, Rebu Hui, 1988.

come when it would not be possible to visit his grave. Also, most of Bruce's immediate family now reside in the United States.

It was a few days after Bruce's death that I returned to Seattle with his body. My friend, Rebu Hui, accompanied me. She kept me sane and I don't know what I would have done without her. I fell asleep immediately on the plane and slept like an unconscious person—my brain had finally shut down. Rebu looked after the kids on the plane, through our stay in Seattle, and many times since. She was mature beyond her years. I was only 28 years of age at the time, Rebu, 22.

Unfortunately, in transit, the casket was scratched. Moisture must have penetrated in some way because when we arrived in Seattle, it was discovered that the color from Bruce's blue suit had infiltrated the white silk lining of the casket and we had to replace it. According to Chinese tradition, this meant that he was not resting peacefully—there was more to be done.

The funeral in Seattle was a much simpler and more sedate affair. It was attended by some hundred invited friends and relatives. The music was not traditional, but consisted of current songs that Bruce liked, including "And When I Die." I can never hear this song without remembering the funeral and the final line which says when I die, there'll be one child born (in this case, two) to carry on. The casket was covered with white, yellow and red flowers making up the yin-yang symbol. The pallbearers were Steve McQueen, Jim Coburn, Dan Inosanto, Taky Kimura, Peter Chin, and Bruce's brother Robert.

Bruce was buried at Lake View Cemetery overlooking the placid waters of Lake Washington which he knew and loved so well. At the funeral, I said that Bruce had viewed death in the following way: "The soul of a man is an embryo in the body of man. The day of death is the day of awakening. The spirit lives on." I added that on "our day of awakening, we will meet him again." Taky said Bruce had "inspired good in others." Ted Ashley spoke of regret at what might have been.

Finally at the gravesite, James Coburn spoke the last words: "Farewell, brother. It has been an honor to share this space in time with you. As a friend and as a teacher, you have given to me, have brought my physical, spiritual and psychological selves together. Thank you. May peace be with you." Then he dropped the white gloves he had worn as a pallbearer into the open grave and the others followed suit.

I returned once more to Hong Kong for the coroner's inquest. I was satisfied that he died of a hypersensitivity to a combination of ingredients contained in Equagesic. I listened to the fanciful theories and heard the speculations grow. The more closely one analyzed these ideas, the more absurd they seemed. They ranged from suggestions that Run Run Shaw had Bruce murdered to suggestions that Raymond Chow had organized it. The truth was

that the people of Hong Kong had lost a great hero and were reluctant to accept the reality that their super-hero could succumb as easily as any other mortal. Amid the onrush of rumors, counter-rumors and lurid assertions, I publicly pleaded to the people of Hong Kong and the world to let the matter alone. "The only thing of importance is that Bruce is gone and will not return. He lives on in our memories and through his films. Please remember him for his genius, his art and the magic he brought to every one of us. I appeal to all of you to please let him rest in peace and do not disturb his soul." No one, I'm sorry to say, seemed to be listening.

I had spent six weeks in Hong Kong attending the inquest and making arrangements to move the house furnishings, and by October I was all set to return to America. I had lived throughout the entire ordeal in a state of seminumbness. Now I looked forward to getting away from Hong Kong, away from all the publicity and the rumors, away from an impossible situation, away from a place where I could not even go out of the house. I was looking ahead to getting back to Seattle, to my children, who had been staying with my sister, to begin facing up to life without Bruce. For six weeks I had been surrounded by friends, by Bruce's relatives, and they had made it as easy for me as possible.

My friend Rebu Hui stayed up all night with me before I left Hong Kong. As I say, I had lived throughout these last few months in a state of semi-shock, semi-numbness. I had gone about doing what had to be done as though I were completely normal and controlled. I had tried to carry on as Bruce would have wished me to. At the time, and even now 15 years after Bruce's death, I can clearly recall the feeling of strength that I experienced during those first weeks. I have never, before or after, felt such concentration of psychic effort within myself. It was a feeling of having to do what was proper for Bruce and for our children. I do not give credit for this feeling of strength to any internal resources within myself, but rather to emanations that continued to radiate from the bond between Bruce and myself. Bruce had relied on me for so much throughout our life together and I was determined to continue in the same way.

It was not until I boarded the plane at Hong Kong airport to take me back to America and a new chapter in my life, that the full impact of what had happened suddenly struck home. Everything flooded in as the numbness fell away as though I had been hit by a paralyzing blow, and I was conscious only of the land falling away below me and the burning tears streaming down my cheeks. Then I remembered lines from the ancient Chinese poet Tzu Yeh (A.D. 265-419) which Bruce had translated:

Young man.
Seize every minute
Of your time.
The days fly by;
Ere long you too
Will grow old.

If you believe me not
See here, in the courtyard
How the frost
Glitters white and cold and cruel
On the grass
That once was green.

Do you not see
That you and I
Are as the branches
Of one tree.
With your rejoicing
Comes my laughter;
With your sadness
Start my tears.

Love,
Could life be otherwise
With you and me?

Bruce once said, "The greatest satisfaction is to hear another unbiased human being whose heart has been touched and honestly says, 'Hey, here is someone real!' I'd like that! In my life, what can you ask for but to be real, to fulfill one's mission and above all actualize one's potential instead of dissipating one's image, which is not real and expending one's vital energy." Without question, Bruce Lee was an incredibly "real" human being, and he shall always reside in the most precious and loving place in my heart.

Bruce's tombstone at Lakeview Cemetery in Seattle, Washington.

13

With few exceptions, none of us travels through the course of our life without having to come face to face with the loss of close friends and loved ones. The reality of death is never easy, to say the least, and often the emotional scars remain with us for years. With some the pain lasts throughout their entire lifetime.

Unquestionably, in the years following Bruce's death I have endured considerable emotional distress, as have our two children. In the beginning I was filled with anger, oftentimes gut-level rage. For a man to work so hard for so many years, achieving some very worthwhile and meaningful goals—goals which meant so much to so many people—only to be taken in the prime of his life neither made any sense, nor seemed fair. Aside from the philosophical, even theological considerations—those deep universal blind alleys as to the very meaning of life that plague us all and more often than not lead absolutely nowhere—there was the more practical aspect to Bruce's death and that was that my children and I deeply missed him and desperately wanted him with us. We needed to hear his laughter, to be enlivened by his incredible energy, most of all we needed his daily wisdom and guidance.

My children and I were not alone in this need, for it was shared by thousands of Bruce's fans and fellow martial artists, and in one sense of the word, I became responsible for their grief as well, which at times served to further compound my own personal anguish. We were all angry, and for a period of time all of us were to one degree or another lost. Yet, in a most peculiar sense, what a wonderful gift it has been to be lost—lost as Bruce, himself, once was. For as Bruce so often said, "A good teacher functions as a pointer of the truth, exposing the student's vulnerability, forcing him to explore himself both internally and externally, and

"Ever since I was a child I have had this instinctive urge for expansion and growth. To me, the function and duty of a quality human being is the sincere and honest development of one's potential."

—Bruce Lee

finally integrating himself with his being." In the course of Bruce's 32 years of life, there is no question but that he did, in fact, totally integrate himself with his own being. In the course of one's own spiritual growth, what more is there for any of us to do?

It has taken the better part of the past 15 years for me to finally come to realize that Bruce's death was not totally in vain, and although I do still have my moments, for the most part I have come to terms with the death of my husband and am today at peace. In reality, Bruce's death exposed me to my own vulnerability, and as a result I, too, was forced to explore myself, by myself. Perhaps the operative word here is "forced." I have not been alone in my travels. Over the years I have received thousands of letters from Bruce's fellow martial artists and close friends who have been forced, in Bruce's absence, to travel similar paths in an effort to find their own reality, to become integrated with their own being. Their resulting personal growth and achievement, for the most part, has been both remarkable and astounding. Surely none of us will ever know for certain, but the question will always remain: "Would we have traveled along these unique and particular paths if Bruce were still alive?" By the same token, I was asked this same question many years ago by a black gentlemen regarding the death of Martin Luther King. Before I could answer, the man smiled and said, "We must have faith. We are not God."

In the course of my own personal growth, I have come to believe that Bruce came to this life with a very definite purpose, and at such time that he accomplished that purpose, he left us all, for a very definite reason. Perhaps it will help to bring peace to many who continue to have difficulty with my husband's death if I elaborate for a few pages on this very point.

I don't believe that it was an accident that Bruce was born into a show business family and that, as a result, he indeed became a child star. Of course, one can say that Bruce was not the only child in the Nathan Road household, so why Bruce? To answer that question one only need recall Bruce's very words spoken at a very early time in his life: "As long as I can remember I feel I have had this great creative and spiritual force within me that is greater than faith, greater than ambition, greater than vision. It is all these combined. My brain becomes magnetized with this dominating force which I hold in my hand." The force to which Bruce referred was a "creative and spiritual force." Looking back over Bruce's life it is clear that he inevitably expressed his extraordinary creativity through the vehicle of motion pictures, while his most significant spiritual growth was destined to take root in the foundations of Chinese kung fu.

I believe it was providence that eventually led Bruce to Professor Yip Man. Had Bruce been a scholarly student and a churchgoer rather than somewhat of a juvenile delinquent, it is doubtful that his life would have taken the course that it did. And so perhaps it was necessary for him to fight in the streets of Hong Kong, for had he not thought it necessary to learn how to defend himself, it is highly improbable that he would have ever taken up the martial arts.

As I have stated previously, Professor Yip Man taught Bruce a great deal more than just physical movements of kung fu. In essence, over the course of five years Bruce became a total martial artist, having learned the spiritual apsect of the art, as well as the deep philosophical teachings of the Far East. This, too, I feel was a very necessary element of Bruce's growth, for this alone labeled him as a unique martial artist. What is of great importance in further understanding the course of Bruce's life is to realize that Bruce as a martial artist was not all that unique in Hong Kong. Although he was unquestionably an excellent student, the salient point is that he was not alone. However, in sharp contrast, upon his arrival in the United States it was clear from the very beginning that he stood in a class all by himself. As Ed Parker once stated, "Bruce was one in two billion." Had Bruce remained in Hong Kong it is likely that he would have continued training with Yip Man for years and probably would have become a senior instructor, but in order for him to realize his own uniqueness, it is clear, in retrospect, that it was necessary for him to travel to the United States. This, too, had been preordained on the day of his birth when his mother named him Lee Jun Fan (Return Again).

Shortly after his arrival in the United States, Bruce wrote, "I feel this great force, this untapped power, this dynamic something with me. This feeling defies description, and no experience with which this feeling may be compared. It is something like a strong emotion mixed with faith, but a lot stronger." Bruce is by no means the first person in history to describe such profound inner manifestations. Many others have come before him and it is certain that many more will follow. What is important is that Bruce, by the time he reached the age of 18, was astutely aware of this extraordinary force within him and was determined not to use it wrongfully. He realized that there was a great purpose to his life, even though at the time he could not clearly envision it. After considerable comtemplation, however, he would soon write, "Ever since I was a child I have had this instinctive urge for expansion and growth. To me, the function and duty of a quality human is the sincere and honest development of one's potential." When he wrote these words, Bruce could not possibly have conceived of what the future held for him, of the incredible heights to which he would rise—that he would become a kind of messiah to his own people—a man worshipped in Hong Kong and in Southeast Asia as the embodiment of all the heroic virtues of the Chinese and other Asian peoples.

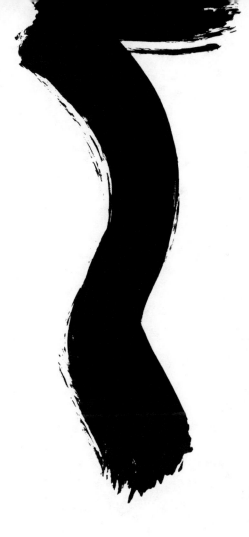

When I first met Bruce, his greatest love was unquestionably the art of Chinese kung fu, and he honestly believed that the major part of his life's purpose was for him to plant the seeds of his beloved art throughout the United States. In pursuit of this most admirable goal, he had a clear idea of how he was going to accomplish such a major undertaking, and how he was going to reconcile his dreams and ambitions and whatever success came his way with the underlying principles of kung fu. Although Bruce did not realize it at the time, his dreams were too small. And as fate would soon dictate, so, apparently, was his art. In essence he had been resting on his laurels for too long. There was considerable more growth necessary. It was about this time that his fight with the alleged kung fu expert occurred. and although Bruce won with considerable ease, the fact that the fight lasted too long caused him to question his own personal expression of kung fu, which ultimately led to the realization that not only was wing chun very limiting but that he, personally, was not in the best of physical condition. And so it was at this time that the first seeds of Bruce's own personal approach to the martial arts were planted. This, too, was a very necessary stepping stone along the path he was traveling, and as a result, he abandoned the notion of opening a chain of kung fu schools. The problem was relatively simple. Ultimately, what Bruce had to offer was far greater than physical martial arts techniques and he very soon realized that he did not have the necessary manpower of instructors to teach his principles to such a vast populace, nor would he ever. And so the journey for the moment hit a brick wall. Somehow, someway, a greater vehicle would have to make its presence known.

The event was Ed Parker's Long Beach Karate Internationals, held in August of 1964, where Bruce gave his first major demonstration of Chinese kung fu. Today that particular exhibition remains a classic, and the raw 8mm footage which recorded it is considered priceless. Of course, it is martial arts history that Bruce's appearance in Long Beach led to his role in *The Green Hornet*. The brick wall had toppled. Bruce now had a vehicle through which he could show a vast television audience his extraordinary talent, at least the physical aspect of it. Although at the time both Bruce and I were saddened by the cancellation of the series, I realize now that had *The Green Hornet* been an overwhelming success, even to the point of syndication, in all likelihood Bruce's genius ultimately would have been "chewed up," as Jim Coburn so wisely, and consistently, warned could happen. Ironically enough, the reruns of *The Green Hornet* planted the first seeds of Bruce's stardom in Hong Kong, although he would have absolutely no idea of this until he one day traveled to Hong Kong, only to be mobbed in the streets by adoring fans. What I see as ironic is the fact that had Bruce realized his growing star status in Hong Kong any sooner than he did, there would have been a great possibility that he would have pursued the Mandarin film circuit far too early.

The Green Hornet was primarily a vehicle which allowed Bruce to display his physical prowess, but did very little, if anything, to exhibit his acting talents. Far more importantly, the series was never designed to delve into kung fu beyond the physical aspect. As a result, I believe that had Bruce gone to Hong Kong at this point, he would not yet have formulated in his mind the rudiments underlying the sheer brilliance he displayed in his films two years later. In the very same sense, his genius could have just as easily been chewed up on the Mandarin film circuit as it could have in episodic television in the States. The timing was critical, there were still forces at work.

About this time there occurred a very specific, and necessary, event which foreshadowed Bruce's inevitable rise to superstardom in Hong Kong. The event I refer to was his severe back injury which took him away from his acting career for a period of six long months. Although Bruce suffered both severe physical pain and mental anguish, these six months were perhaps the most creative period in his life, for it was during this time that the *Tao of Jeet Kune Do* was written, and hence his deep and profound thoughts on the martial arts became etched in stone forever. Had this writing not taken place at this particular time, it may well have never been done. In light of the remarkable success of this massive literary work, and all the good it has brought to so many seekers, it is clear that such a work had to be written. Yet, not only did it have to be written for thousands of others who would read it again and again in the future, but Bruce needed to write it for himself, for his own personal growth. With the completion of the *Tao of Jeet Kune Do*, Bruce had formulated in his mind all of the thoughts he would later fight so desperately to reveal in his films.

Following Bruce's recovery from his back injury, he would travel to Hong Kong to visit his relatives, only to discover that he had achieved the status of a star. Upon his return he would film the television episode of *Longstreet*, wherein for the first time he was able to show the deeper human aspect of his beloved art. With the show's overwhelming success, coupled with the fact that he was now being approached by producers in Hong Kong, Bruce soon made the following prophecy:

"I, Bruce Lee, will be the highest paid Oriental superstar in the United States. In return I will give the most exciting performances and render the best of quality in capacity of an actor. Starting in 1970, I will achieve world fame and from then onward till the end of 1980 I will have in my possession $10,000,000—then, I will live the way I please and achieve inner harmony and happiness."

One of the misconceptions about my husband is that he could

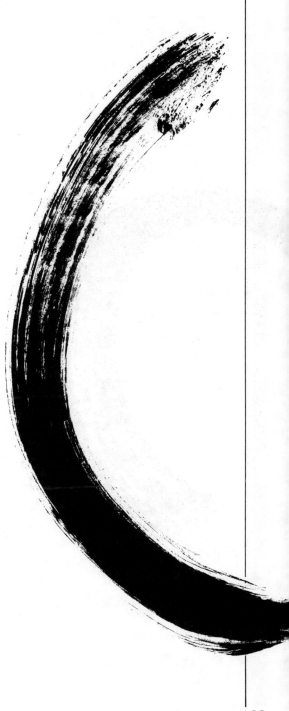

not help becoming a success because he was blessed with such considerable natural talent. Of course, he had talent, but it has always seemed to me that not enough attention has been paid to how hard Bruce worked to improve and perfect all his abilities. He trained as hard as any martial artist I have ever known or heard about. In this regard, I know that millions of his fans are convinced that Bruce was born with a special body, yet many of them simply do not believe it when I explain that Bruce built up his outstanding physique through sheer application and will power and through intense training.

By the same token he flung himself into the art of acting with a concentration that only a man who burned up energy like a furnace could achieve. In his vast book collection, there were many volumes on acting, which he studied assiduously. Talent is supposed to find its own outlets, create its own opportunities. Yet antithetically, in Bruce's case, it has always seemed to me that he was driven by a sheer desire to not only create his own opportunities, but to, at the same time, constantly improve his own talents.

Some of his old friends, such as Stirling Silliphant, hold the view that Bruce, instead of extracting that calmness and tranquility from the martial arts that is a part of teaching of Zen Buddhism, found only conflict and antagonisms, adding that Bruce "invited a lot of these slings that kept coming back at him." This, of course, is to misinterpret the whole nature of Bruce's philosophy and outlook. Harmony is the interaction of yin and yang. In his search for greater and greater achievement, he was following one of the oldest and more constructive forces within mankind. During the last two years of his life, Bruce was having a difficult time dealing with people who were not genuine. It simply was not in his nature to believe that people were purposefully trying to injure him. He was very sensitive and attuned to human feelings, and I think in time he would have "yinned" more and "yanged" less. But at this particular time in his life, he was still learning and growing. *The Silent Flute* itself contained many of the themes that reflected Bruce's life and behavior at this time. The script traced a young student's evolution through the martial arts, his problems of ego, his newfound courage in facing the abyss of death, and finally his spiritual rebirth. At one point Bruce says in the script, "I'm not even sure what trials I passed through—or how I came to be here. I still have doubts, many doubts. . . how, without more struggle, can I resolve them?"

In those last two years, Bruce often came home from the studios very boisterous, wrought-up, highly charged about whatever the problem happened to be at that moment. When he was at the studios and something was going wrong, he used to telephone and ask me to come over. I don't think I ever did much to alleviate the situation but I was a steady base for him, something he knew would not waver even when everything else was getting to him. On the whole I believe we each did what was required of us in relation to the other. We played our separate roles as best we could and perhaps surprised each other by surpassing expectations we had never felt justified in entertaining, for as Bruce often quoted, "I'm not in this world to live up to your expectations and you're not in this world to live up to mine." Although I always had a total confidence in him, even I, in the end, found that he had more than lived up to my most secret hopes.

Bruce's life was a growing process. He was a man of great depth, one who could sit meditatively for long periods of time, and then write down his reflections thus:

"I am learning to understand rather than immediately judge or to be judged. I cannot blindly follow the crowd and accept their approach. I will not allow myself to indulge in the usual manipulating game of role creation. Fortunately for me, my self-knowledge has transcended that and I have come to understand that life is best to be lived and not to be conceptualized. I am happy because I am daily growing and am honestly not knowing where the limit lies. To be certain, every day there can be a revelation or a new discovery. I treasure the memory of the past misfortunes. It has added more to my bank of fortitude.

"My first love is martial art. By martial art, I mean an unrestricted athletic expression of an individual soul. Martial art also means daily hermit-like physical training to upgrade or maintain one's quality. To live is to express one's self freely in creation. Creation, I must say, is not a fixed something or a solidification. So I hope my fellow martial artists will open up and be transparently real and I wish them well in their own process of finding their cause."

When I read Bruce's words about his hermit-like existence in order to achieve merit and quality, I think of the many nights I awoke in the small hours and found my husband, his restless mind and energies still burning so fiercely that he could not sleep, busy working at his desk or training at his art, striving to drive his mind and body toward new goals that only he could perceive, goals that he realized could never come any nearer, for as he reached one new level of perfection, another still lay ahead of him. Had he lived, I'm sure he would have found an inner contentment based on his philosophy of life.

Bruce's main goal was never to be wealthy or famous but to produce quality work. And, in the end, he managed to arrange his life so that it became like his jeet kune do—simple, direct, effective. In fighting, he achieved this by never being bound by rules or limitations—indeed, he made the slogan of his institute: "Using no way as way; having no limitations as limitation." He used to insist when instructing his pupils, "Efficiency is anything that scores"—and in living, efficiency meant to him to be clear-thinking, always making sure that his thoughts were directed toward purposeful action. To Bruce it was wrong to wish without moving or to move without having a specific aim.

Bruce was never orthodox but, in sharp contrast, always the innovator. When he began to teach, for example, he disdained the typical ranking system of belts. Belts, he used to say, are useful for holding up your pants! A few years later, when he had become a nationwide celebrity, he was asked by an interviewer if there were any rankings in kung fu. He replied, "Not in traditional kung fu—however, we have a unique ranking system in our particular method. Actually, (and here his intense brown eyes began to twinkle) I should say a ranking system of no ranking. The first rank is a blank circle, which signifies original freedom. The second rank is green and white in the form of the yin/yang symbol with two curved arrows around it. The third is purple and white, the fourth is gray and white, the fifth is red and white, the sixth is gold and white, the seventh is red and gold, which is our school's emblem, and the eighth rank is the highest, which is a blank circle, the return to the beginning stage. In other words all the previous rank are only good for cleaning up messes. "I think it extremely noteworthy that Bruce's life, in essence, followed the very course of his belt system in jeet kune do. In a sense, he made a full circle, beginning as a young man in Hong Kong whose life to one degree or another a mess, then to have attained world fame through his remarkable achievement, only to return to Hong Kong, with new understanding, in the end. Perhaps to some this is providence.

Bruce, in so many senses the very essence of physical fitness, a man almost totally absorbed with his body and extraordinary abilities, subconsciously felt a strong sense of urgency to get a great many things done in a short space of time. A unique artist and a legend in his own lifetime—not only worshipped as a hero on the silver screen, but revered by practitioners of the martial arts the world over for his expertise off the screen—was well on his way to becoming one of the highest paid actors in films. He was the first Asian superstar to bridge the chasm between East and West, to contradict the outrageous stereotypes represented on film and TV by such "Chinese" figures as Charlie Chan and Dr. Fu Manchu. He had, therefore, become a hero to millions in Southeast Asia who identified with him and saw him as their champion. And it is a measure of what Bruce achieved that he managed to destroy that ancient and prejudiced image and, instead, ultimately projected an image of a Chinese who, for once, was not only a hero but one with whom Western audiences could identify. He stood at the helm and not only made the whole world conscious of his beloved art of kung fu, but at the same time raised the status of his own people, as well as the quality of

Chinese films. Tantamount to all else, however, through his work and his writings, he gave us all a realistic approach to life, essentially giving us the necessary tools with which we might ultimately find ourselves and live up to our God-given potential. Bruce was truly a man of great purpose.

Looking back on my husband's life, perhaps one of the most interesting aspects of all is the way he grew, matured, and blossomed in so many different ways—physically, mentally, and spiritually. The truly remarkable essence of Bruce's life is not the skills he achieved, nor the money he made, nor the fame he created. The greatest achievement is what he made of himself. Physically, he turned a skinny, delicate frame into a marvelous tool. Mentally he gave to us remarkable, deep wisdom. However, I truly believe that on a spiritual level he made his greatest and most profound strides ever.

The words of Jhoon Rhee seem appropriate as a final comment: "Bruce was a man of victory."

14

A whole cult has grown up around Bruce—and I think it will continue to grow bigger rather than die away.

Although from a historical standpoint Bruce died on July 20, 1973, little did I know at that time that many years after his death his name would be even greater and more widely known than when he was alive, that like earlier legendary screen figures such as Rudolph Valentino and James Dean who had died at an early age, Bruce would become the nexus of a world cult.

In addition to the scores upon scores of magazine and newspaper articles, books, films, tributes, martial arts tournaments and posthumous awards given in Bruce's honor, I, personally, have received thousands upon thousands of letters from Bruce's adoring fans and dedicated martial artists. Equally as touching to me are the hundreds of others who pay annual visits, often traveling great distances, to lay flowers and other mementos at Bruce's gravesite in Seattle.

Of course, as is always the case surrounding the early death of an international superstar of Bruce's prominence, there are those who have questioned his death, as well as others who have started rumors or made statements regarding his life. Understandably, I feel a deep responsibility to Bruce and his fans to briefly address a few of these issues.

Without a doubt, the most widely asked question which has been addressed to me over the years has been "How did Bruce Lee die?" Amidst an assortment of sensationalistic speculation ranging from fatal gunshot wounds to a deranged individual using psychic powers to kill Bruce from a darkened room across the street, I personally believe the findings of the distinguished panel of physicians who extensively, and quite thoroughly, examined Bruce's body over the several days immediately following his death. As stated at the official inquest in Hong Kong, these individuals unanimously agreed that Bruce died from a hypersensitive reaction to one of several compounds contained in the drug Equagesic, which is a standard remedy prescribed for mild pain such as might be symptomatic of a common headache. Chemically Bruce's body had an adverse reaction to the ingestion of this drug, thereby causing what is known as edema (the collection of fluid) in his brain. As a result, he merely went to sleep and, following a brief span of time, peaceably died.

Perhaps the second biggest issue which surfaced in the wake of Bruce's death was an assortment of erroneous dialogue regarding his formal training. Whether attributed to a lust for financial gain or to bolster their own personal esteem in the martial arts, over the years, scores of individuals have made statements to the effect that they to one degree or another taught Bruce. In the interest of historically setting the record straight, Bruce officially was taught by only one master, the late Professor Yip Man, who was an expert in the Chinese art of wing chun. Upon his departure from Hong Kong in 1959, Bruce never again became a student of any other master, nor did he pursue the teachings of any particular or exclusive martial arts system or style.

To those who are knowledgeable in the martial arts, the obvious question surfaces—If Bruce only studied wing chun, then where did jeet kune do come from? The answer is quite simple. Jeet kune do (JKD) was Bruce's own personal expression of his own personal martial art, the foundation of which he absorbed by physically investigating numerous systems, as well as spending countless hours reading several thousand texts on the combative arts of judo, aikido, karate, kung fu, wrestling, savate, Western and Thai boxing and fencing, in addition to an equally impressive number of both ancient and modern texts on a wide assortment of martial arts weaponry.

To complete the full picture, there were three highly esteemed martial artists with whom Bruce spent extensive quality time exchanging ideas—Ed Parker, Jhoon Rhee, and the late James Lee. Both collectively and individually these men shared a mutual respect and admiration for one another, and I am quite certain that they all gained from their close personal, as well as professional, friendships. In addition to these three men, Bruce did learn the finer points of grappling from judo expert Gene LaBell, and was taught the basic movements of the Filipino double sticks *(nunchaku)* by his close friend and student Dan Inosanto. Moreover, there were numerous other prominent martial artists with whom Bruce spent a lesser degree of time, primarily on the level of a teacher, the most noteworthy of whom were Chuck Norris, Joe Lewis, and Mike Stone. In the final analysis, and over the

In these photos, Grace, Brandon, Shannon and I appeared at the premiere of the remake of The Game of Death. Pictured on the left is Norman Borine, a devoted follower of Bruce.

Bruce's older brother Peter.

course of many years, Bruce ultimately arrived at a functional and very personal martial art by "taking what was useful and rejecting what was useless."

In a somewhat related subject, over the years there have been those who have made the statement that they had fought and beat Bruce. This is simply not true. With few exceptions, this type of statement has come from relatively unknown martial artists, most of whom never knew Bruce and certainly never made such statements while Bruce was alive.

In addition, since Bruce's death there has been a handful of derogatory books and articles written about Bruce, essentially by opportunistic authors who clearly did not do their homework, but instead, for the most part, relied on third and fourth party hearsay. Moreover, there have been film producers and actors who have capitalized on Bruce's name and likeness for their own financial gain. Throughout the years I have been approached by individuals who have stated that they recently saw Bruce on television or on a movie screen, only to stare in puzzlement upon learning that who they saw was not Bruce. From a factual standpoint, Bruce only made four films—*The Big Boss, Fist of Fury, Way of the Dragon,* and lastly, *Enter the Dragon.* Regardless of the motives of these individuals who have to one degree or another profited from their endeavors, I believe it is a credit to Bruce's years of hard work and his subsequent international popularity which allowed them to do so.

One of Bruce's main goals in life was to spread his beloved art of kung fu throughout the Western world and I feel it important to give the readers a general summary of the path jeet kune do has taken since Bruce's death.

As could well be expected, Bruce's assistant JKD instructors were stunned by the death of their master, and in the beginning there was much reorganization to be done in Bruce's absence. Initially the torch was placed in the hand of Bruce's senior student Dan Inosanto, who has to this day played a major part in carrying on where Bruce left off. Soon after Bruce's death Dan was approached by several groups of substantial businessmen who offered to finance the opening of nationwide franchises using Bruce's name. Of course, in that Dan was well-known as Bruce's senior student, he was to spearhead the proposed, and quite massive, organization. However, as Bruce had also done in previous years, Dan very flatly, and very quickly, turned them down. In truth there is no question but that Dan could have prospered considerably had he pursued such offers, and I think it is a credit to his integrity and honest friendship with Bruce that he has insisted on keeping JKD on a low profile and directed his attentions to quality rather than to his own personal financial gain.

Another of Bruce's original assistant instructors, actually his first, is Taky Kimura, who still lives in Seattle and continues to teach a small group of dedicated martial artists in the ways of Jun Fan kung fu. Like Dan, Taky could have prospered by exploiting his association with Bruce, but he, also, understands that Bruce's way of martial arts was a gift that he and Bruce shared. Taky continues to be a dear friend of our family. He generously shares his very busy life with those who come seeking "the way" in hopes that they can absorb the philosophical message of Bruce's martial arts as well as the physical.

Today the foundations and concepts of JKD can be found in the teachings offered at the IMB Academy in Carson, California. The Academy is headed by one of Bruce's old students, Richard Bustillo, who is the director and co-founder, as well as Dan Inosanto and Chuck Martinez, who trained with Richard and currently is the Academy's president. In the interest of keeping close to the continuation of Bruce's work, I personally remain on the Jeet Kune Do Society's Board of Directors and offer my time and counsel whenever called upon. In addition to the teachings of Lee Jun Fan Gung Fu, the Academy offers expert instruction in muay Thai, tai chi chuan, (yang style), kali, Western boxing, and grappling. In connection with the IMB Academy, an affiliated school, which is run by Dan Inosanto, is located in Marina del Rey, California. As a credit to the growth of JKD, other affiliated schools are located in England, Scotland, Germany, Spain, Japan, and Australia, as well as in numerous locations in the United States. Dan Inosanto, Richard Bustillo, and Larry Hartsell are also in high demand on the international martial arts seminar circuit. Readers having questions as to accredited instructors and locations of seminars are encouraged to contact the IMB Academy located at 305 West Torrance Boulevard, Carson, California 90745.

Bruce's sister Agnes.

Of course, in reality it is highly impractical that the tens of thousands of martial artist interested in pursuing Bruce's teachings can enroll at the few schools in existence. For this reason alone, years ago I authorized the publication of a portion of Bruce's writings which can be found in the *Tao of Jeet Kune Do*. As of this date the *Tao of JKD* is currently in its eleventh printing and is distributed internationally in five different languages. Again, the incredible popularity of this book, as well as the several volumes of *Bruce Lee's Fighting Method,* is further credit to Bruce's countless hours of hard work and sincere dedication to his most beloved art, and there is no doubt that Bruce would be most pleased by the fruits of his endeavors which have greatly enriched the lives of so many.

Bruce is held in such high regard by his fellow martial artists

Bruce's sister Phoebe.

Bruce's younger brother Robert.

that there is now an annual tournament held in his honor in Fort Worth, Texas. It is called the Bruce Lee Scholarship Tournament and is sponsored by Richard Morris. Originally the brainchild of tae kwon do grandmaster Jhoon Rhee, the goal of this unique competition is to award a college scholarship to the high school martial artist who excels in three areas: *kata* (forms), sparring, and scholastic grades, as evidenced by the fact that those who compete for the scholarship must qualify by having a B average. I (and in 1988 my daughter Shannon) have attended this tournament every year and spoken to the many young people about Bruce's love of books, his self-disciplined study habits, and the progress he made in his art through self-education. It has always been my goal, and it is one of the purposes of this book, to tell people as much about Bruce's philosophies as about his movies and his martial arts. I am sure Bruce would be honored to know that through this tournament he continues to be an inspiration to young men and women, especially when it concerns improvement of the mind as well as the body.

Bruce used to tell interviewers that his first love was always martial arts while acting was simply his profession. But those of us who were close to Bruce knew that his first love was always his family. Over the years we have all changed and grown, and there is no doubt that our lives have all been different than they might otherwise have been had we not been touched by Bruce's life as well as by his death. This is perhaps an opportune time to comment briefly on the lives of those who were near and dear to Bruce.

Bruce's mother, Grace, came to live in the United States in the early 1970s when Bruce was able to help her enter this country because of his U.S. citizenship. For a time she moved between her daughter Phoebe's home in San Francisco and our home in Los Angeles. When Bruce and I moved to Hong Kong in 1971, Grace and Bruce's younger brother Robert moved to the San Gabriel Valley, California, where they continue to live to this day. Grace was gravely affected by Bruce's death and she had a hard time understanding how her beautiful, healthy son could die at such an early age. But over the years her deep wounds have healed and she has been most gracious in granting interviews and making appearances on her son's behalf, being very proud of Bruce's achievements and his status in the world. Grace is in good health and happy and has assumed her place as the matriarch of the Lee family. We have been able to see her frequently over the years, and she has always taken a great interest in the well-being of Bruce's children. It brings a tear to her eye when she sees the many similar characteristics between Bruce and Shannon.

Bruce's two sisters both live in the United States and are doing well. Phoebe, the oldest of the Lee children, lives in San Francisco, yet visits Los Angeles quite often to see her mother and family. A woman of fierce family pride, she probably knows more about the Lee family history than anyone else and, like Grace, has been generous in granting interviews to those seeking to tell Bruce's life story. On past occasions, it has angered her when journalists have not been fair or truthful and, as a result, she has learned, like the rest of us, to be discriminating in granting such interviews.

Agnes, Bruce's second older sister, attended school in the San Francisco Bay area when Bruce and I lived in Oakland. We were able to see her often in those days and she was a great help to me when Brandon was born. Agnes and her husband, Bing, now live in Long Island, New York, where she is a hospital lab technician, in addition to having raised three children. I had not seen Agnes for many years until recently, when she visited the West Coast for a family reunion. We hope to be able to get together more often so that our children can continue to grow together.

Peter, Bruce's older brother, attended college in Minnesota where he excelled in physics. After his father's death in 1965, Peter returned to live in Hong Kong. Today he holds a prominent position with the Hong Kong Royal Observatory. When Bruce and I lived in Hong Kong, from 1971 to 1973, we were able to see Peter and his family quite often, and I have visited him when I have traveled there in the years since.

Bruce and brother Peter.

Robert, Bruce's younger brother, came to live with us in the early 70s when we lived in Los Angeles. Before Robert left Hong Kong, he was a popular singer, and he and his band appeared in many nightclubs. He gave up this promising career to come to the United States to complete his education at California State University at Los Angeles. Robert now lives in the Los Angeles area where he has an interest in a restaurant and nightclub, in addition to assuming the role as chief caretaker of his mother. Like the other members of the family, Robert has shown his pride in his brother by speaking openly and truthfully to people who have wanted information about Bruce.

In addition to the jeet kune do family mentioned earlier, there are a few martial artists who were so close to Bruce that I consider them more friends than colleagues. Jhoon Rhee, the tae kwon do grandmaster from Washington, D.C., spent countless hours in our home as we did in his. He and his wife, Hahn Soon, have remained good friends of mine and my children, and have always sought to promote Bruce's image in a positive light. For over three decades, Jhoon has remained a powerful force in the martial arts. He has tremendous

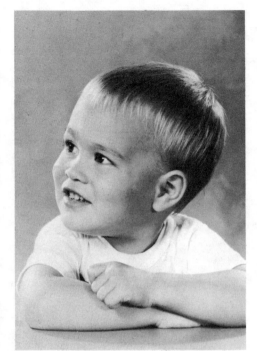

Brandon—the only grey-eyed, blond-haired Chinaman in the world, according to his father.

Brandon mugs for the camera—a born ham.

energy, both physical and spiritual, and the loftiest of goals in promoting strength, truth, and knowledge through the martial way. The World Martial Arts Congress for Education was Jhoon's inspiration and the Bruce Lee Scholarship Tournament exists chiefly through his efforts. I look forward to a lifelong association with Jhoon Rhee and his family.

Ed Parker, the "father of American karate," is another dear and long-time friend of our family. He was one of the first martial artists Bruce knew in the United States and was instrumental in introducing and legitimizing Bruce to other prominent individuals in the arts. It was chiefly because of Ed that Bruce obtained his first role in American television, the part of Kato in *The Green Hornet*. Since Bruce's death, Ed's celebrity status in the arts has singled him out to those interested in Bruce. As was the case with Dan Inosanto, there were several instances wherein Ed could have prospered financially by capitalizing on his close friendship with Bruce, however chose not to. He is a man of true integrity and it is rare in today's world that we find men of such stature. Earlier this year, I attended a long overdue tribute to Ed Parker, produced by Tom Bleecker, one of Ed's first generation black belts. When Ed went to the podium at the close of the event, he was most gracious in acknowledging Bruce as a leader and innovator in the arts. My family and I enjoy socializing with Ed and his charming wife, Leilani, often trading stories about the early days. As with the Rhee family, a friendship exists with the Parkers that goes far deeper than our martial arts connection.

James Lee was the first martial artist that Bruce became friends with in the United States in 1959. When Bruce moved to Seattle to attend the University of Washington, he and James were in constant contact and each traveled to the other's place of residence to practice and confer. When Bruce and I were married in 1964, we moved to James' house in Oakland where we lived for most of the next year. Bruce and James founded the second branch of the Jun Fan Gung Fu Institute on Broadway in Oakland. As has been related earlier, when James' wife died unexpectedly, Bruce and I became "aunt" and "uncle" to James' children Greglon and Karena. Later, when Bruce and I moved to Los Angeles and later to Hong Kong, the two men were constantly in touch. Sometime in the early 70s, James contracted cancer and his life became truly a battle. He was always so excited about Bruce's success and was looking forward to coming to Hong Kong for the premiere of Bruce's film, *The Way of the Dragon,* at the end of 1972. Unfortunately, James died just before he was to leave for Hong Kong. It was a major blow to Bruce who was beginning to experience a shortage of real friends in the Far

East. Over the years, I have remained friends with Greg and Karena and have always said they were my first "children" because they were in my care even before Brandon and Shannon were born.

Another friend and student of Bruce's is Peter Chin. I can't remember how long I have known Peter—it seems like he was always there. After Bruce's death, Peter spent long hours with me, each of us consoling the other, trying to figure out the impossible whys and what nows. I have always been grateful for his friendship in those days. Peter now lives in Las Vegas with his wife Sandy and their two children. He is currently planning a spectacular tribute to Bruce and the martial arts, even traveling to China in the hope of persuading the Shaolin Temple to send representatives. Peter felt deeply influenced by Bruce, not only in the arts, but by his personal philosophy for living, and in his own way, has tried to show the world the worth of the man.

Lastly, there are Bruce's and my children, Brandon and Shannon.

Brandon was born on February 1, 1965, at the East Oakland Hospital. Bruce was intensely proud to have a son, the first grandchild in the family. I should have known there was trouble on the horizon when Brandon blasted his way into this world at a healthy eight pounds, 11 ounces. Due in part to his mother's inexperience and our frequent moves, Brandon did not sleep through the night for 18 months. He never took to a pacifier or a special blanket, he just hollered all the time, which ironically, seems to have marked the beginning to his life's pattern.

Brandon was born with a head of jet black hair which quickly fell out and grew in platinum blond. Bruce used to say that Brandon was the only grey-eyed, blond-haired Chinaman in the world. Bruce's father was equally proud to have a grandchild and Bruce was happy that his father knew of Brandon's birth because Lee Hoi Chuen died only one week after Brandon was born. Bruce was a super dad, but he was not the kind who changed diapers or got up in the middle of the night. He had weightier things on his mind, like building a career and paying the bills.

When we lived in Los Angeles, Brandon not only had in his eyes the greatest dad in the neighborhood, but unquestionably the scariest. He had a friend, Luke, with whom he played frequently, but Luke never liked to come to our house to play. It took some months before I discovered from Luke's mother that her son was afraid of Brandon's dad and the kung fu practicing, equipment banging, and the menacing looking weapons that were common sights and sounds in our backyard.

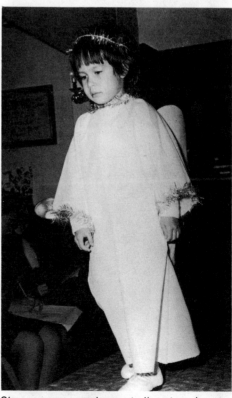

Shannon—an angel came to live at our house.

Younger brother Robert Lee.

When we moved to Hong Kong, we entered a different world. Children there are shepherded everywhere they go because the city is so crowded and threatening. Brandon attended La Salle College as Bruce had as a child. The students were all Chinese, but the classes were taught by Catholic brothers in English. Consequently, Brandon learned to speak Cantonese fluently by playing with the other school children. In the first and second grades, Brandon was in a class of 50 students who shared desks and only attended half a day. He did so well that when we returned to the United States, he was able to skip the third grade.

Bruce and Brandon were very close. They played together, practiced kung fu together, traveled together, and read books together. Brandon was eight years old when Bruce died. To explain to this child that the hero of his life could no longer come home, was incomprehensible to him. After the traditional Chinese funeral in Hong Kong, we returned home to Seattle where we had another funeral and Bruce was buried. So many things happened so fast that the kids got a fast shuffle. I was called back to Hong Kong for the coroner's inquest and had to leave my children with my sister in Canada for three months. It was hard for them to understand why they were suddenly parentless for this extended time. Thanks to my sister, Joan, they survived with psyches intact.

We eventually settled down in Seattle where we thought we would pick up a normal life-style. It was not in the cards. Since *Enter the Dragon* had not been released in the United States before Bruce's death, we were unprepared for the sudden impact Bruce would have on the world. It was especially hard for Brandon. He had not only lost his father, but now he had to contend with the publicity that ensued. Brandon was trying to work out his own personal hurt, and trying hard to be the man in the house for his mother and sister, and he was only eight. As a result, he became a very private person and kept his feelings to himself. He didn't like to talk about his father because he felt it made me feel sad. He had trouble with friends who would repeat rumors they had heard about Bruce. But he would never tell me—he just dealt with it.

In 1974 we moved to Los Angeles where Brandon attended one school continuously for the first time in his life and began to display his own personality. He became a leader at school, a quality sometimes frowned upon by teachers and administrators. He finally had one teacher for the sixth, seventh, and eighth grades, Mr. Montgomery Waters, who related well to Brandon's intellectual, oftentimes rebellious, makeup.

Brandon has always caused me to ponder the age-old question of genetics versus environment. Like his father, he never had a leaning toward science or math, but excelled in reading, writing, and public speaking. In high school, Brandon was active in the performing arts. He loved to write and came under the wing of his English and drama instructor, Mrs. Karen Stephens. As a senior he was elected student body president, but the innovations he had in mind for the school did not fit in with the administration's mind set.

At a very early age, Brandon clearly defined his life goals and, as a result, upon graduating high school pursued a course of higher education at Emerson College in Boston where he studied acting and traveled frequently to New York for acting lessons.

Today Brandon persists in seeking his own truth and his own unique spotlight in the world. As a working actor he has made several films and television appearances. At the time of this writing he is about to commence filming an action-adventure feature film. Aside from the superficial pomp and circumstance which often envelops the life of children of famous parents, Brandon is sincerely and deeply proud to be Bruce's son. At the same time, to his credit, he insists on retaining his own identity and fulfilling his own destiny. Most important of all, today I have a 23-year-old son who is my friend, and who wants as much happiness for me as I want for him.

Our daughter, Shannon, was born April 19, 1969, at Santa Monica General Hospital when we lived in West Los Angeles. From the time Bruce found out I was pregnant, he expressed the hope that our second child would also be a boy because he felt that he could relate better to male children. But when Shannon was born, a ladylike six pounds, six ounces, it was as if an angel had come to live at our house. Bruce was absolutely delighted in a way he had never expected. Little girls always win their daddy's heart, and it was no different in the case of Bruce and Shannon, who truly was the apple of her father's eye.

Brandon and Shannon, ages six and two.

As much as Brandon had been the tough little guy who was a walking disaster area—broken leg, broken arm twice, fractured skull, to name just the major accidents—Shannon was a delicate flower of a child with physical problems of her own. She had a rough time from the beginning. Her foot was turned the wrong way, which resulted in her being fitted with an orthopedic brace between both feet from the age of nine months. Blessed with the determination of her father, however, she soon could swing herself out of the crib and crawl all over the house before she was even old enough to walk.

After we moved to Hong Kong, she began to have problems with her eyes. Eventually she underwent eye surgery to straighten her eye muscles—an unnerving experience for a

A 1988 photo of the Lee family: Phoebe, Grace, Agnes, Robert, and family friend Nancy Choy.

three year old to wake up and not be able to see for a week—and for her parents as well. When at last we thought all her physical problems were solved, Shannon began to lose her hearing. This condition got alternately better and worse for several years until she finally had her tonsils and adenoids removed at age seven. Since those early years, Shannon has had no further infirmaries, and has grown and developed into a beautiful young lady. These were not major problems on the grand scope of things, but I mention them because these were trying times for Bruce as he struggled to make a success of his film career. It is no wonder he became terribly protective of his children.

When we lived in Hong Kong, Shannon was between the ages of two and four. She attended a Chinese nursery school, but it was not the same as we consider nursery school in this country. Because of the fierce competition to enter a first-rate elementary school in Hong Kong, preprimary education also becomes very competitive. When Shannon attended school at age three, she wore a uniform, carried a book bag and was required to learn Chinese reading, writing and speaking. She did very well and, like Brandon, still retains the foundations of the Cantonese language. After our return to California, Shannon attended Chinese school on Saturdays for many years so that she would not lose her knowledge of the language and culture.

Bruce died when Shannon had just turned four years old. She has very little recollection of what was going on around her at the time of her father's death. Even today, she does not remember a great deal about her father, which to me is understandable, in that my own father died when I was five and I, too, can only recall brief glimpses of his presence. Though she may not have specific memories of Bruce, the majority of Shannon's personality and temperament were formed during those crucial first four years when her father was alive. As he had with Brandon, Bruce spent a great deal of time with his daughter, playing, reading, and snuggling. He was very close to both of his children and loved them very much. Shannon and Brandon were a great solace to Bruce, and they, in turn gave him their unconditional love. Ultimately they provided a purpose for his life goals.

Shannon is an excellent student, but like Bruce and Brandon, she does not have an affinity for technical subjects, but instead, leans toward the performing arts. Fortunately, in elementary school, she was also under the tutelage of Mr. Waters who pushed her through the nitty gritty stuff of mathematics and science. Shannon's true essence began to blossom in high school, where she performed in several musicals. She is blessed with a vocal quality that even I did not realize she possessed. Genetically speaking, I certainly cannot understand where she inherited this talent since I can't sing at all and Bruce used to joke that he had a "rich voice"—it was "well-off."

Today, Shannon attends Tulane University in New Orleans where she is studying voice. She has appeared in several shows, and we look forward to seeing her in many more. Whether she ultimately decides to pursue this as a career will be her decision, but for the present she is dedicating herself to developing her musical gifts. Both Brandon and Shannon have always been low-key about their relationship to their famous dad, and are seeking to prove themselves on their own merit.

Even though Shannon does not remember her father well, his presence has surrounded her life. As she has gotten older, she has taken on the fierce pride which is typical of this family and is currently spearheading the effort to persuade the Hollywood Chamber of Commerce to place a star on the sidewalk for her father.

Shannon has always been a child who had empathized deeply with her mother. As a young person she was uncharacteristically concerned about my well-being. Even as a teenager she would defer going out with friends if she thought I would be lonely at home. She does not make judgments quickly and reserves her opinions about others. Today Shannon is a lovely person whose friendship I value beyond the fact that she is my daughter.

Finally, there is me. I have truly had a blessed life. Having two wonderful, healthy, and happy children would, in itself, be enough. But I always consider it my fortune that I was able to be married to Bruce, to know him in that very unique relationship. Because our marriage was so intimate, I knew his every mood and instinct. I counted on him for his uncanny insights into people, for his strength against adversity, and for his courage against odds, truly "grace under pressure."

Bruce's death was total devastation to me. But shortly after the moment of his passing, I felt a flow of energy between us that I believe was a result of our closeness in life. I can only say that I experienced a clarity of mind and purpose that I wanted to deny but could not. While Bruce was alive I was often publicly cast as his shadow, but with his death I was infused with a strength that I believe was his gift to me.

When Bruce died, his last movie *Enter the Dragon* had not yet been released in the United States. About one month after his death I attended the premiere of his film at Grauman's Chinese Theater in Hollywood. I had asked our friends at Warner Brothers to "do it right for Bruce," and they surely did just that. It was truly spectacular, but not easy to watch

Bruce's children grow up.

Pictured with members of the Jeet Kune Do Society: Herb Jackson, Tim Tackett, Richard Bustillo, Larry Hartsell, Jerry Poteet, Daniel Lee and Ted Wong.

my husband on the screen full of vitality, realizing he could not be present to enjoy his success.

There have been difficult times over these years. It took me a long time to realize that not everyone is as well intentioned about Bruce as I am. In the early years, I was very hurt when I read articles about Bruce that were untrue. I used to write lengthy letters to newspaper and magazine publishers when they printed falsehoods about Bruce's life. I was shocked when so-called biographical films were released which were not only untrue but sensationalized. It took a long time for me to understand that the legal questions presented in this area were often insurmountable. Not only are there First Amendment issues involved, but I did not realize that when a person dies, he surrenders any rights of privacy he may have possessed while alive. Through it all, however, often against seemingly unbeatable odds, my lawyer, Adrian Marshall, has worked assiduously to protect Bruce and my rights and those of the children. There have been times when I wished that Bruce's life could be free of controversy, but over the years I have accepted the fact that Bruce's life and death will remain a mystery to those who are searching in the wrong direction.

Ultimately, I have been able to give my life a healthy direction. I do not linger on past hurts, but instead, today enjoy great happiness. It is my philosophy that personal contentment is not necessarily a day to day happening, but a general feeling of well-being within oneself.

After Bruce died, I returned to live in Seattle, my hometown, where I thought I would settle with my children. Bruce is buried in Seattle at Lakeview Cemetery that overlooks Lake Washington. He was happiest when he lived in the Pacific Northwest and we often talked about having a home there in the future. However, at least in my case, it has never been truer that "you can't go back," and so, after a year of missing the southern sunshine, I moved back to Los Angeles.

Bruce died without having drawn a will. We had not considered the possibility of his passing away at such a young age. Regardless, the complications resulting from this oversight proved to be long lasting and it took seven years to probate Bruce's estate, requiring numerous trips to Hong Kong to deal with governmental authorities.

During this time, I attended college to obtain the degree I had begun at the University of Washington many years earlier. Finally at age 36, I received my Bachelor's degree in Political Science at California State University at Long Beach. It had been my intention to go on to law school, but by this time I felt this was too contentious a life-style for my personality, and so as an alternative I went to work as a receptionist-secretary at the school Shannon and Brandon had attended during their elementary years. I continued to attend school at night to obtain my teaching credential, and I now teach kindergarten in the Los Angeles area. It is a productive pursuit and one which gives me boundless pleasure.

Brandon and Shannon are now well-grown and have essentially moved out of the family home. My mother joined me in California after she retired from Sears in Seattle, and she and my stepfather, Willard, live nearby. My mom has been a great help to me through all the years of raising the children and taking care of the house, and even greater, we are friends and she has always been my main cheerleader.

I have been a most fortunate woman, a fact that I have never taken for granted. Bruce was tremendously influential in carving out the person I am today. In addition, through a lot of love from my children, my mother, my aunts, uncles and cousins, my rudder has always been stabilized. As a result, today I know who I am and what I do best to add to a better world. Ultimately and in the final analysis, this continues to bring me much happiness.

Shannon and Brandon.

189

MORE BRUCE LEE BOOKS FROM OHARA

TAO OF JEET KUNE DO
  by Bruce Lee. Code No. 401

BRUCE LEE'S FIGHTING METHOD, Vol. 1, Self-Defense Techniques,
  by Bruce Lee and M. Uyehara. Code No. 402

BRUCE LEE'S FIGHTING METHOD, Vol. 2, Basic Training,
  by Bruce Lee and M. Uyehara. Code No. 403

BRUCE LEE'S FIGHTING METHOD, Vol. 3, Skill in Techniques,
  by Bruce Lee and M. Uyehara. Code No. 404

BRUCE LEE'S FIGHTING METHOD, Vol. 4, Advanced Techniques,
  by Bruce Lee and M. Uyehara. Code No. 405

CHINESE GUNG FU,
  by Bruce Lee. Code No. 451

THE LEGENDARY BRUCE LEE,
  by the Editors of BLACK BELT. Code No. 446

BRUCE LEE MEMORIAL BOOK,
  with introduction by Linda Lee. Code No. X904

Ask for free catalog:
OHARA 🔲 PUBLICATIONS, INC., 1813 Victory Place, P.O. Box 7728, Burbank,
California 91510-7728   1-800-423-2874